Contents

Notes on contributors

Dr Will Bartlett is a Senior Lecturer in the School for Policy Studies at the University of Bristol and co-director (with Teresa Rees) of the project 'Guidance services and the learning society' which is part of the ESRC's *Learning Society Programme*.

Dr Andrew Burns is a Research Fellow at the Centre for Continuing Education at Edinburgh University, and is completing a doctorate in politics. He previously worked in personnel for several years.

Dr Antje Cockrill is a Research Associate in the Centre for Advanced Studies in the Social Sciences and a tutor in the School of Education, University of Wales, Cardiff. She recently completed a doctoral thesis at the University of Wales, Aberystwyth.

Professor Frank Coffield has been Professor of Education in the Department of Education at the University of Newcastle since April 1996, having previously worked at Durham and Keele Universities. He is currently Director of the ESRC's research programme into *The Learning Society* from 1994 to 2000. In 1997 he edited *A national strategy for lifelong learning*, Newcastle, Department of Education, University of Newcastle.

Ms Isabelle Darmon is a member of the research team at the Tavistock Institute, London, studying 'Innovations in continuing vocational training: a comparative perspective' as one of the 14 projects which make up the ESRC's *Learning Society Programme*.

Ms Pat Davies is Director of the Continuing Education Research Unit at City University and she also directs the project 'The impact of credit-based

learning systems on learning cultures', which is part of the ESRC's *Learning Society Programme*.

Mr Carlos Frade graduated in the Universidad Autonoma of Madrid and in 1992 he joined the scientific staff of the Tavistock Institute.

Dr John Fitz is a Senior Lecturer in the School of Education, University of Wales, Cardiff and a member of the research team studying 'Training for multi-skilling: a comparison of British and German experience', one of the projects in the ESRC's *Learning Society Programme*.

Ms Kari Hadjivassiliou is a member of the research team at the Tavistock Institute, London, studying 'Innovations in continuing vocational training: a comparative perspective'; one of the 14 projects which make up the ESRC's *Learning Society Programme*.

Professor Walter Heinz is Professor of Sociology and Social Psychology and Director of the Life Course Centre (Special Research Centre of the German Research Council, DFG) at the Universität Bremen, Germany. He is a visiting Professor at Canadian and US universities. His main research interests are education and work, socialisation and the life course and cross-national cultural studies.

Ms Cathy Howieson is a Senior Research Fellow at the Centre for Educational Sociology at the University of Edinburgh. She is currently taking part in a comparative study of academic and vocational education in England, Wales and Scotland as part of the ESRC's *Learning Society Programme*.

Professor David Raffe is Professor of Sociology of Education and Director of the Centre for Educational Sociology at the University of Edinburgh. He has conducted several 'home international' comparisons of the home countries of the UK, comparative studies of European and other OECD countries, and is a co-director (with Michael Young) of the Unified Learning Project, which is part of the ESRC's *Learning Society Programme*.

Professor Teresa Rees is Professor of Labour Market Studies in the School for Policy Studies at the University of Bristol and co-director (with Will Bartlett) of the project 'Guidance services and the learning society', which is part of the ESRC's *Learning Society Programme*. Recent publications include *Women and the labour market* (Routledge, 1992); *Women and the EC training programmes: Tinkering, tailoring, transforming* (SAUS Publications, 1995).

Dr Peter Scott is currently Lecturer in Employee Relations in the Department of Management at Manchester Metropolitan University. He has also worked at the Universities of Bath, Bristol, West of England and the University of Wales, Cardiff, where he was a researcher on the project reported in this volume. His research interests include vocational training within Europe, skills and work organisations, and European public sector trade unions.

Professor Tom Schuller is Director of the Centre for Continuing Education at the University of Edinburgh. Recent publications include *The changing university* (ed, Open University Press, 1995) and *Part-time higher education: Policy, practice and experience* (with David Raffe et al, Jessica Kingsley, 1998). He is co-director (with John Field, University of Warwick) of a project within the ESRC's *Learning Society Programme* entitled, 'Divergence between initial and continuing education in Scotland and Northern Ireland'.

Mr Ken Spours is a Researcher at the Post-Sixteen Research Centre at the London Institute of Education.

Professor Michael Young is Professor of Education and Director of the Post-Sixteen Research Centre at the London Institute of Education. He is co-director (with David Raffe) of the Unified Learning Project, which is part of the ESRC's *Learning Society Programme*.

Introduction: lifelong learning as a new form of social control?

Frank Coffield

Introduction

Mr Podsnap's world was not a very large world, morally; no, nor even geographically: seeing that although his business was sustained upon commerce with other countries, he considered other countries, with that important reservation, a mistake, and of their manners and customs would conclusively observe, 'Not English!' when, PRESTO! with a flourish of the arm, and a flush of the face, they were swept away. (Dickens, 1952, p 128)

The United Kingdom's relationship with the rest of the world has never been easy and Podsnapian attitudes have not vanished from British politics or British society. But, as other members of the European Union continue to integrate (by, for instance, adopting a single currency), and as the models developed for the future of Europe by the European Commission become more numerous and detailed, the case becomes ever stronger for increasing the flow of independent, critical and *comparative* research into policy, practice and performance in all the member states of Europe. For example, the European Commission in a recent communication has decided to build "a Europe of Knowledge", as one of the "fundamental pillars of the Union's internal policies" (CEC, 1997, p 16). There is an implicit assumption in the communication that we all understand and agree on what is meant by the term 'knowledge'. No definition is offered and the nearest comment to a definition is the remark that "the citizens of Europe will be able to develop their fund of knowledge continually, thus expanding and renewing it on a lasting basis" (CEC, 1997, p 3).

In this regard, it is instructive that the European Commission's White Paper, published in 1995, on *Teaching and learning* was subtitled *Towards The Learning Society* in English, but *Vers la Société Cognitive* in French and *Auf dem Weg zur Kognitiven Gesellschaft* in German. Whether the switch from the French and German emphasis on 'knowledge' to 'learning' in the English version is an indication of a significant cultural difference in approach and in values depends on how the two words are defined and used. If, for example, our European partners mean by 'knowledge' the centrality of new theories as *the* source of innovation, while 'learning' is being interpreted in the UK as the opportunity to accumulate credits, then the choice of words becomes crucial. It is by no means clear, however, what the definition of 'knowledge' is in these European reports, but one gets a sense of it being used in a new way which is close to the view of the Office of Science and Technology (OST) in London, which describes the task of universities as one of "turning their products into acceptable consumer packages" (OST, 1995, p 38).

In a world where the official terminology which is used has the power to influence policy, thinking and the distribution of funds to the creators and users of knowledge, a sociological imagination of the kind possessed by Basil Bernstein is needed to capture the essence of this new definition of knowledge and of the modern divorce of knowledge from the knower:

Knowledge should flow like money wherever it can create advantage and profit. Indeed knowledge is not like money, it is money. Knowledge is divorced from persons, their commitments, their personal dedications.... Moving knowledge about, or even creating it, should not be more difficult than moving and regulating money. Knowledge, after nearly a thousand years, is divorced from inwardness and literally dehumanized. (Bernstein, 1996, p 87; emphasis as in original)

This collection of seven articles explores and, at times, deconstructs such central notions in the public discourse over the future of Europe as 'lifelong learning', the 'learning organisation' and the 'learning society' by drawing on a series of comparative studies, which are part of the Economic and Social Research Council's (ESRC) *Learning Society Programme*. Some of the chapters which follow also present considered reflections on the purposes, processes and pitfalls of comparative research in the social sciences; some chapters, and especially the first (an invited contribution from Walter Heinz of Bremen University), do both, while other chapters employ comparison as a means of expanding the understanding of the substantive topic under investigation.

The present volume is the second in a series of reports to be published by The Policy Press over the next two years on such themes as skill formation (the topic of the first report[1]), research and policy, and informal learning. The *Learning Society Programme* has already produced a contribution to the debate on lifelong learning, entitled *A national strategy for lifelong learning* (Coffield, 1997) and a collection of articles, which explored the concept of a learning society, in a special edition of the *Journal of Education Policy* (vol 12, no 5, November-December 1997). This report presents some further empirical findings and theoretical insights which have begun to flow from the 14 projects which make up the programme.

It may be appropriate to begin by briefly introducing *The Learning Society Programme* itself. The full title of the programme is '*The Learning Society: Knowledge and skills for employment*' and the original specification described it as follows:

The programme is a response to the growing national consensus that the UK needs to transform radically its thinking and practice in relation to education and training if it is to survive as a major economic power with a high quality of life, political freedom and social justice for all its citizens.

The aim of the programme is to examine the nature of what has been called a learning society and to explore the ways in which it can contribute to the development of knowledge and skills for employment and other areas of adult life. The programme focuses on post-compulsory education, training and continuing education in a wide variety of contexts, both formal and informal.

The programme consists of 14 projects, involving over 50 researchers in teams spread throughout the UK, from Belfast to Brighton. Each project has a different starting and finishing time and the programme itself will run until March 2000. The six projects which present papers in this collection constitute a subgroup with a substantial comparative dimension to their research design; it is also important to note that they are reporting early or interim findings of a tentative nature in the following chapters rather than firm conclusions which are to be published at a later stage[2].

The rest of this introduction will concentrate on five large themes which recur throughout the seven chapters: the political context within which comparative research in the UK is conducted; the pleasures and pains of such research; the significance of language in cross-national work; different models of *The Learning Society*; and, to ensure a sting in the tail, lifelong learning viewed as a new form of social control. But before turning to these themes, it is worth making clear the very wide range of issues and the different types of comparison which are covered by the seven contributions to this volume.

Walter Heinz, for instance, contrasts the German version of lifelong learning with those current in the UK, the USA and Canada. He offers an alternative, sceptical interpretation of the concept to that advocated by the official rhetoric in all these countries, and his dissenting interpretation provides a better explanation of the high levels of non-participation in continuous learning in both Germany and the UK. In Chapter 2, Teresa Rees and Will Bartlett argue that views of a learning society need to move beyond an "overly simplistic and deterministic link between improvements in skill and the achievement of more rapid economic growth" to a consideration of other models. In all, they describe three different models of a learning society and their different implications for guidance services and, in particular, they contrast such services in the Netherlands with those in England, Scotland, France, Germany and Italy. Chapter 3 compares innovations in continuous vocational training within firms in three countries – Britain, France and Spain. Isabelle Darmon, Carlos Frade and Kari Hadjivassiliou show how each country has developed a different form of *'social compromise'* between the drive for competitiveness through market values and those social forces seeking to protect employees from the excesses of de-regulation. In Chapter 4 Pat Davies compares two credit-based systems of learning – one in London and the other in the Nord/Pas de Calais regions of France, both of which are attempts to increase participation by adults traditionally under-represented in education and training and with no or few qualifications. The study reported in the final chapter by Antje Cockrill, Peter Scott and John Fitz involves another intra-European comparison of multi-skilling in three different economic sectors (engineering, construction and residential care) in South Wales and two German regions, Nordrhein-Westfalen and Baden-Wuerttenberg.

The two remaining chapters are rather different in approach in that both are 'home internationals' rather than comparisons between countries within the EU, that is, the focus is on comparing systems *within* the UK[3]. Tom Schuller and Andrew Burns, for example, are intrigued by the apparent discrepancy between, on the one hand, relatively high rates of participation and achievement in *initial* education in both Scotland and Northern Ireland as compared to equivalent rates in England and, on the other hand, lower rates in both countries in *continuing* education, again in comparison with rates in England. An international flavour to this study is, however, provided by a panel of correspondents from seven countries, who are commenting upon the conceptual framework and the empirical findings. Finally, David Raffe, Cathy Howieson, Ken Spours and Michael Young compare developments in policy on post-compulsory education and training in Scotland with those in England and Wales. Again, this project is complemented by the involvement of the research team in a European study across eight countries of strategies to promote parity of esteem between vocational and academic learning in post-16 education. What all the contributors have in common is a desire to learn from cross-national observations which perforce involve them in all the pleasures and pains of comparative studies, which have been commented on by a long line of distinguished researchers such as Brian Holmes, Sig Prais and Hilary Steedman.

The political context of comparative research in the UK

It is now seven years since Ewart Keep noted the strong inclination in the national debate in the UK about education, training and employment "to compare and contrast British practice with that of our overseas competitors" (Keep, 1991, p 23) and British practice has on the whole fared badly in such comparisons. Since then the grass has continued to look greener, particularly in Asia until, that is, the economic and social crises of 1998 in South Korea, Thailand and Indonesia, for instance. Such unforeseen outcomes have, however, only served to fuel the debate about what can and cannot be learned from such comparisons (see Reynolds and Farrell, 1996). A number of educational and economic reasons have been offered for the sudden increase in international traffic in comparative studies. For Andy Green the most influential has been "the intensification of economic competition between nations and the perception by governments the world over of the importance of education and training for economic advance" (1997, p 173). For example, the Conservative administration of Mr John Major became so concerned about the competitiveness of British industry that it commissioned a *skills audit* in 1996 to examine the UK's comparative performance on basic qualifications for employment with four competitor countries – France, Germany, the United States and Singapore. The report, published jointly by the Department for Education and Employment (DfEE) and the Cabinet Office as a mark of its importance to the thinking of central government, argued as follows:

... with the increasing international mobility of other factors of production, so that capital and management skills can now be brought in more easily from abroad, a country's economic performance arguably now depends more on the (relatively immobile) human capital of its population than it has done in the past.... As a result, education and training may now be becoming more

important determinants of a country's rate of economic growth. (DfEE/Cabinet Office, 1996, para 2.14)

The dependence on the comforting ideology of human capital which deflects attention away from structure and on to individuals is criticised at length elsewhere (see Coffield, 1997, p 4). The next crucial stage in the argument is to demonstrate how or to what extent levels of skill determine productivity or competitiveness, but instead of developing a causal chain of explanation, the link is simply assumed:

It has not been the purpose of this audit to explore how skill levels are related to competitiveness; we have taken that as given. (DfEE/Cabinet Office, 1996, para 1.3)

The election of the new Labour government in 1997 created the possibility of a clean break with this dangerously oversimplified and seriously incomplete account of the relations between education and employment. Indeed, the Foreword to the government's Green Paper on lifelong learning, written by the Secretary of State, David Blunkett, acknowledges that learning has a wider contribution to make beyond securing our economic future:

[Learning] helps make ours a civilised society, develops the spiritual side of our lives and promotes active citizenship. Learning enables people to play a full part in their community. It strengthens the family, the neighbourhood and consequently the nation. It helps us fulfil our potential and opens doors to a love of music, art and literature. That is why we value learning for its own sake as well as for the equality of opportunity it brings. (DfEE, 1998, p 7)

In addition, the new administration quickly embraced the language and thinking (which other European governments have fought hard to place high on the political agenda), of *social exclusion* and established a Social Exclusion Unit.

So far so good. But a closer reading of the Green Paper suggests a ministerial determination to increase individual employability as *the* central policy in the development of lifelong learning. An indication of that determination can be found when the Green Paper turns from rhetoric in favour of lifelong learning to a discussion of practical measures. The policy of previous Conservative governments, for instance, which refused student loans to those over 50, is not to be reversed: "We do not think it would be appropriate to make income-contingent loans available to students who do not plan to re-enter the labour market" (DfEE, 1998, para 2.22). This surely suggests that the main, if not the only purpose of learning, is to prepare people for employment. So much for the claim of valuing learning for its own sake!

The unease created by such instrumental thinking is not assuaged by the words of the new Labour Prime Minister, Mr Tony Blair, who reduces a complex debate to the simple sound-bite: "Education is the best economic policy we have" (DfEE, 1998, p 9). In other words, education has been "publicly redefined as a mere instrument of the economy", as the researchers from the Tavistock Institute put it in Chapter 3 of this collection. One outcome can be fairly confidently predicted: questions from politicians about what the British can learn or borrow from the education and economic systems of other countries are likely to become more insistent. All the more reason for researchers to have well-rehearsed arguments about the limitations as well as the strengths of such international comparisons.

The pleasures and pains of comparative research
Limitations

The standard warning in the literature argues that the direct transfer of policy or practice, whether wholly or in part, from one country to another is likely to prove ineffective if not impossible. There is also the danger of simply misunderstanding what is happening in another society by, for instance, studying methods of teaching without an appreciation of the cultural and intellectual traditions surrounding teaching and learning in that country (see Gipps, 1996). And when an area has become politically sensitive, it becomes necessary at times to question "the ways in which cultural strangers on flying visits interpret what they think they see" (Chisholm, 1987, p 157), in case superficial and potentially damaging conclusions are drawn. In the literature, such dangers are ritually acknowledged but Isabelle Darmon and her colleagues in Chapter 3 of this report seek to avoid them by arguing that a transnational comparison of education and training policies needs to begin by examining wider political, economic and social policies, together with the regulatory framework:

> *Too often such comparative exercises are mere mechanical juxtapositions, and seem to be, perhaps unwittingly, underpinned by an axiom that elements or components of innovations have meaning and function in themselves, that is, independently of the* **configuration** *within which such components are included. To this atomistic view we wish to oppose a* **systemic view** *according to which* **the relationships between innovation components and the system within which such components function is far more important than the components taken by themselves.** *(Chapter 3, emphasis as in original)*

Pat Davies rightly adds in Chapter 4 the necessity of a deep understanding of the historical development of the systems under study.

A good example of the importance of structural differences in international comparisons is given by Antje Cockrill, Peter Scott and John Fitz in Chapter 7. Superficially, the role of the German Chambers of Industry and Commerce (*Industrie- und Handelskammer*, IHK) may appear similar to that of the English or Welsh Training and Enterprise Councils (TECs), especially after the merger of some TECs with their local Chambers of Commerce, but the differences run much deeper: "The IHK organisations play a central role in the German training system, enjoy a symbiotic relationship with local firms through the system of membership and levies that apply, and are far more powerful than their British counterparts" (Chapter 7).

A further practical difficulty concerns timing. Two of the chapters discuss the problems of establishing relationships between systems which are not only changing and moving in different directions, but are also at different stages of development. Cathy Howieson and David Raffe were, for instance, interviewing policy makers in Scotland at a time when the main strategic decisions had already been taken, whereas in England, Ken Spours and Michael Young were conducting interviews when the basic strategy itself was still under discussion. Similarly, the study of multi-skilling in South Wales and two regions of Germany had to cope with the fact that

during fieldwork the three regions were at different stages of the economic cycle, with South Wales emerging slowly from recession, while Baden-Wuerttenberg was beginning to feel the effects of a recession more dramatically than Nordrhein-Westfalen (see Chapter 7).

Furthermore, Walter Heinz shows in Chapter 1 how international comparisons of participation rates or skill levels are inherently very difficult. Part of the problem consists in establishing *equivalencies* between qualifications in different countries and careful empirical research has documented that, for instance, "it is even more difficult to make comparable codings for educational attainment and the variety of lifelong learning arrangements than achieving comparable codings for class origin" (Chapter 1). National classification systems such as age and socioeconomic categories embody pre-conceived ideas which differ from country to country, as Annette Jobert, Catherine Marry and Lucie Tanguy point out (1997, p 1). At one level, then, equivalence in cross-cultural research involves researchers developing comparable meanings for key concepts and agreeing definitions of the indicators to be used to operationalise them. But, as John Bynner and Lynne Chisholm argue, "a deeper, and perhaps even more challenging, set of issues resides in the origination of comparative study and the motivations of those who undertake it ... who is making the comparison and for what purpose?" (Bynner and Chisholm, 1998, pp 132-8).

Advantages

Cross-national comparisons can at their best challenge, and perhaps even puncture, national myths which tend to feed on confirmatory, but which seek to ignore contradictory, evidence. That is certainly the case with the myth that has given rise to the title of this report, namely, that the strength of beer is thought to be positively correlated with northern latitudes, a belief which simultaneously evokes the stereotype of the effete southerner. Walter Heinz in Chapter 1 questions the new myth of 'the learning organisation', while David Raffe has previously challenged the enduring myth of Scottish education as "broad, accessible, democratic, meritocratic and communally oriented, particularly compared to England" (1991, p 48). But Tom Schuller and Andrew Burns' research in

Chapter 5 indicates the danger of complacency: "the very success of Scottish *initial* education, or at least its successful reputation, may limit people's awareness of the need for *continuing* education" (emphasis added). Interestingly, David Raffe and his colleagues in this volume refer to that infuriating smugness in the British character (summed up in Scotland by the phrase "wha's like us? Damn few and they're aw deid!"), when they write: "there is a reluctance, in both England and Scotland, to accept that anything could possibly be learnt from developments on the other side of the Border" (see Chapter 6). How likely is it, then, that British politicians, policy makers or professionals could find it in themselves to learn from *Spain*, where, for instance, the principle of solidarity has been translated into political action by the introduction in 1992 of a tax on both employers and employees which devotes 50% of the funds to the training of the unemployed (see Chapter 3)?

It is also highly instructive to see ourselves as others see us. Walter Heinz in the first chapter, for instance, describes the renewed interest in lifelong learning in the UK and in North America as a "substitute for the failure to develop an organised and publicly regulated system of initial vocational education".

The other chapters suggest a wide range of purposes for comparative studies from identifying best practice, to developing new concepts or frameworks in order to describe variation among systems, and to testing theory in different contexts. It is also liberating to review a broader range of policy options, political decisions and particular practices and to realise that similar pressures on all countries from the global market or technological advances do not inexorably produce homogeneous domestic responses – there *are* choices to be made, despite what previous Conservative ministers claimed[4]. The Joseph Rowntree Foundation's *Inquiry into Income and Wealth*, for instance, examined trends in income inequality in 18 countries and found that there had not been a universal trend towards greater inequality and that inequality had, in fact, *fallen* in such countries as Italy, Finland, Denmark and Canada. The main conclusion of the inquiry was that: "Internationally, the UK was exceptional in the pace and extent of the increase in inequality in the 1980s" (1995, p 14).

Perhaps the greatest value of qualitative research in comparative studies is that it throws up new insights and new issues for debate, policy and subsequent empirical investigation. A detailed study of the contrasts and similarities between the system you have been brought up in and its counterpart abroad may make clear as never before the surprising strengths and the unacknowledged weaknesses, the overall shape and the future possibilities of the system you have become too familiar with. It may also be necessary for British researchers to study education and training systems in other countries before they see beyond the similarity of institutional structures and terminology in the UK systems and so come to recognise the essential differences between them. In the words of David Raffe and colleagues, "comparisons which only look within the UK may fail to identify the essential features of 'Britishness' – so, too, many comparisons in which Britain or the UK is represented only by England" (see Chapter 6).

Analysis

Most of the projects reporting in this volume discuss the difficulty in attributing causality, which is not an issue confined to comparative studies, although it is particularly acute within international comparisons because of the additional levels of analysis. Various authors in this report emphasise levels of analysis which are of especial importance to their particular study, but, if all those mentioned are brought together, they constitute a formidable list: international trends in global markets, changing methods of production and technological innovation; European policy; national policy; the historical, social and economic contexts of particular policies; the institutional fabric of the education and training system; the structure of occupations and of labour markets; cultural traditions at national, regional and local levels; strategies adopted by particular sectors or companies; and, last, but not least, individual strategies. There may be researchers who would wish to add to this list of nine levels but understanding how they interconnect within a system over time is what is significant, not their number.

A particular example, which does not draw on all these interacting levels of complexity but which remains an intriguing and important puzzle, is provided by Pat Davies in Chapter 4. Are the statistics of rapidly increasing rates of participation in credit-based programmes in both London and Northern France to be interpreted as the result of the pulling power of courses based on credit, or of the accompanying financial incentives, or of the successful targeting of appropriate students, or of some combination of these and perhaps other factors? As the students are, in the main, unaware of the credit-based nature of the courses and have little or no understanding of how a credit system works before they register, it is unlikely to be the credit system which has attracted them in the first place, but perhaps it is partly responsible for helping to *retain* them. Interviews which are currently being carried out with students will help to disentangle the various pushes and pulls which make up students' motivation to join and complete courses, but no simple causal connections are likely to emerge.

Methodology

There are two main contrasts within the methods adopted by the six *Learning Society* projects represented in this volume. Four of the chapters describe international comparisons while two constitute 'home internationals', which have the following advantage: many of the contexts (historical, social, political, economic, linguistic and cultural) tend to be more similar between England and Scotland than, say, between the UK and Spain.

As some mention has already been made of 'home internationals', the second main contrast will be emphasised here – the decision *either* to subcontract the collection of foreign data to an indigenously-based team of local experts *or* to use the same research team to carry out the fieldwork both at home and abroad *or* to collaborate closely with foreign research partners. Teresa Rees and Will Bartlett (Chapter 2) adopted the third approach; Antje Cockrill, Peter Scott and John Fitz (Chapter 7) and Pat Davies (Chapter 4) the second; and no one used the first approach. According to Antje Cockrill and her colleagues, the main drawback in subcontracting data collection "is the loss of external insight and fresh perspective on social phenomena which is surely one of the very purposes in undertaking" comparative research; on the other hand, the practical difficulties in organising, say, a

hundred interviews in Germany from a Welsh base, even by a native-born German speaker, are not to be underestimated. In support of their approach, Teresa Rees and Will Bartlett argue that UK researchers are unlikely to have as deep an insight into the distinctive institutional environment and political context as the research partners they worked closely with in each of the four countries studied. Those who are planning such research may wish to learn from the mistakes made and from the practical suggestions for future improvements detailed in these chapters as well as from the model collaborative strategies developed by John Bynner and Lynne Chisholm (1998), from their extensive and insightful overview of methodological problems in comparative research. Their exhortation to English-speaking researchers to immerse themselves in the international literature emanating from language cultures other than their own brings us neatly to the next subsection. For the aim is "not only to extend the base of our comparative data, but to gain access to the widest possible range of conceptual apparatus and methodological understandings" (Bynner and Chisholm, 1998, p 143).

The significance of language

The nationalist claim is that full belonging, the warm sensation that people understand not merely what you say but what you mean, can only come when you are among your own people in your native land. (Ignatieff, 1994, p 7)

Given the deservedly poor reputation that the British in general have acquired as linguists, it is perhaps not very surprising how little discussion there is in the research literature in the UK on comparative studies about the problems of language, about understanding the tacit codes of people who are not our own. The significance of language can be gauged from the fact that, among all our friends, colleagues, relatives and acquaintances who are fellow native speakers of English, there are not many of whom we are prepared to say that "we speak the same language".

Linguistic problems do not disappear even if one is fluent in the foreign language and fully immersed in the general cultural and political contexts and in the specific terminology of the research topic. For example, certain concepts are simply untranslatable, as Antje Cockrill et al found with the English term which was the central focus of their research, namely, 'multi-skilling'. They had to employ two German phrases, each of which conveyed slightly different connotations, but which together tried to offer psychological equivalence. Misunderstandings can also be caused (and precious time lost) by the same words having different meanings in the two languages. John Bynner and Lynne Chisholm provide pertinent examples of the *incommensurability* of key concepts:

> The French term **insertion** and **précarité** translate badly into English, in that both arise from a set of specific understandings and practices concerning the mutual rights and responsibilities between state and citizenry in the French polity. In the case of **insertion**, the term 'integration' is too imprecise, and the phrase 'entry to employment' is too detached from the idea of an expectation for an active role played by the state in enabling entry to employment to occur. (Bynner and Chisholm, 1998, pp 135-6)

This general point is intensified when the basic concepts which make up the discourse of lifelong learning such as 'competence', 'key qualifications' and 'skills' not only differ in meaning from one country to the next but also change in meaning *within* any one country over time and are often differently interpreted in different parts of that country at one and the same time. In short, concepts have long (and often controversial) histories in particular places (see Temple, 1997). It also takes time to appreciate all the rich connotations with which a foreign word like *Bildung* is imbued – culture, refinement, and scholarliness are all needed at times to convey the sense of the word rather than just the straightforward translation of 'education'. And what should one read into the French phrase for continuous assessment – 'contrôle continu'?

Moreover, the deliberate avoidance of particular and apparently obvious words in translation can often alert the reader to different ways of looking at the world or to different political stances to controversial issues. For instance, in the European Commission's White Paper on *Teaching and learning: Towards The Learning Society* (1995), the English

version proposes two 'solutions' which education and training can offer to cope with what are seen as the major factors of upheaval (internationalisation of trade, the information society and the relentless march of science and technology) and these are given as: "broad-based knowledge and employability" (p 6). In both French and German the 'responses' from education and training appear to be rather different, '*culture générale et aptitude à l'emploi*' and '*Allgemeinbildung und Eignung zur Beschäftigung*'. Even the adjective 'flexible' is unacceptable in French and so 'a more flexible approach to employment' becomes '*une approche plus souple*'. In the deliberate preference for certain words over others, what becomes clear is the French resistance to an interpretation of 'flexibility' which argues that workers should simply accept whatever wages and conditions their employers think economic – and it is exactly these different national responses to common global trends which are explored by Isabelle Darmon and her colleagues in Chapter 3.

Different modes of a learning society

One of the central aims of the ESRC's *Learning Society Programme* is to develop the concept of a learning society, and Teresa Rees and Will Bartlett do precisely that at the start of the second chapter by suggesting that the term can be viewed in three separate and contrasting ways, which help to place and make sense of the myriad debates surrounding the phrase. The first version which they present currently dominates the official rhetoric in most countries and is called, by them, *the skill growth model*. This argues that the accumulation of skills and knowledge and "the ability to re-skill and re-train the labour force ... is held to distinguish the more successful economies from the less successful". Some commentators consider the assumed link between upskilling and economic prosperity to be dangerously oversimplified and deterministic and therefore prefer the second approach – *the personal development model*, which argues for "an increase in capacities to achieve individual self-fulfilment in all spheres of life, not just in economic activities". Again, those critics, who think it unlikely that a learning *society* will ever be established by developing *individuals*, offer a third model – *social learning* – which celebrates social capital (networks, communications and the strength of civil society) rather than human capital (education and training) and which emphasises "the role of institutions of trust and cooperation in promoting economic growth on an equitable basis". These three models are a convenient device for making sense not only of much of the research conducted by the 14 projects which make up *The Learning Society Programme*, but also of the new Labour government's vision for lifelong learning, as detailed in *The Learning Age* (DfEE, 1998). The Green Paper draws theoretical ideas and policy suggestions from all three models and in doing so moves well beyond the plans of previous Conservative administrations to turn the UK into the Hong Kong of Europe.

There remains, however, one sceptical (if not heretical) viewpoint, and that fourth model, which goes beyond the thinking of the three models described above, will be the final theme of this Introduction.

Lifelong learning as a new form of social control?

The great problem of social order is how to achieve a degree of organisation, [change] and regulation consistent with certain moral and political principles (for example, 'democracy' or 'civil rights') and without an excessive degree of purely coercive control. (Cohen, 1985, p 5)

Over the last 20 years in the English-speaking world, a consensual and dominant rhetoric has been propagated with evangelical fervour about the need for nothing short of a 'revolution' or 'quantum leap' to maintain competitiveness and economic prosperity. This remarkable consensus is publicly celebrated by government and opposition spokesmen, leaders of business and of the trade unions, professional organisations, academic specialists and voluntary groups. Lifelong learning has been chosen by them, like some new wonder drug, as *the* solution to a wide range of economic, social and political problems which include:

- national competitiveness
- the management of industrial and technological change

- employability for individuals
- social exclusion
- active citizenship
- personal fulfilment
- and the quality of life.

The potential of lifelong learning to transform individuals, businesses, communities and whole nations is viewed as limitless, as can be judged from one quotation out of many possible from the new Labour government's Green Paper *The Learning Age*:

> *In communities affected by rapid economic change and industrial restructuring, learning builds local capacity to respond to this change. For the nation, learning is essential to a strong economy and an inclusive society. In offering a way out of dependency and low expectation, it lies at the heart of the Government's welfare reform programme. (DfEE, 1998, p 11)*

These extravagant claims are presented as self-evident truths for which no supporting evidence is required. Lifelong learning apparently possesses all these remarkable powers and still contrives to remain "one of life's pleasures" (Kennedy, 1997, p 1), so much so that the National Campaign for Learning claimed in one of its Newsletters that one of its surveys had found that "More people in Britain would rather go back to school than have sex" (1996, p 1). On this evidence, a revolutionary change in attitudes to the joys of learning should prove an easy and perhaps even an exciting task, but leaves unexplained the high levels of non-participation in lifelong learning. Surveys of more nationally representative samples conducted by Naomi Sargant et al (1997), for example, report that more than half (55%) of their adult respondents say that "they are very or fairly unlikely to take up any learning in the future" (1997, p vii).

Such unreflective hyperbole from the proponents of lifelong learning was likely to create some critical reaction and minority voices began to be heard in the UK objecting to education being restricted to "fulfilling the requirements of the economy under conditions of global competition" (Usher and Edwards, quoted by Green, 1997, p 171). It is precisely in this regard that cross-national observations of the same master concept – in this case, lifelong learning – can reveal fascinatingly different responses by different societies.

Walter Heinz, for instance, in the first chapter shows how the German version of lifelong learning varies markedly from the dominant view taken of it in English-speaking countries. Pointing to the widespread discrepancy between the rhetoric of lifelong learning and the reluctance of German employers to invest in training for *all* their employees, Walter Heinz argues that "In Germany, lifelong learning is contested terrain between employers, unions, [Further Education] FE providers and the state". Furthermore, he detects a hidden agenda behind the ubiquitous rhetoric: lifelong learning is being turned into a moral obligation and an external constraint – "It becomes a normative expectation to participate in recurrent, additional or sequential learning whenever the internal or external job market calls for adjustments ... it socialises people to become more flexible or more employable without promising them job security".

This perspective sees lifelong learning as a means by which individuals are being encouraged to adapt to changing management demands and job requirements, demands which continue to escalate. The level of commitment expected of the modern employee can be gauged from a public statement of a representative of the Swedish Employers' Federation at an international conference on lifelong learning:

> *It is not enough to use the hands and feet of our employed, we must engage their brains and even their hearts. (Lindholm, 1998)*

It is no longer sufficient for employees to internalise the goals of the company; they must learn to love it also. If, however, management's demands for continuous learning are widely viewed as an unacceptable intensification of workloads, then it is not at all surprising that "not even half of the employed population in Germany has participated in any kind of further education". Moreover, in Germany the highly publicised movement which promotes the spread of the learning organisation has to be contrasted with the fact that only 4% of employees report experiences of learning in quality circles or workshops. The reasons given by the non-participants are instructive: two thirds thought that

Further Education would not "lead to improvements in the content and conditions of work" and the second reason was fear of additional stress. In contrast to Germany, in the market societies of the UK, USA and Canada the problems of unemployment, job security and the need for continuous training are being privatised and handed over to individuals (and their families) to solve, as Walter Heinz puts it: "At least for the UK and North America the slogan 'let them eat skills' is changing to 'let them buy skills' with their own money". In Germany, and in France (according to Isabelle Darmon and her colleagues in Chapter 3) there is growing resistance by employees to be treated as the company's "social software", to use Walter Heinz's graphic phrase.

Such views from continental Europe may be considered to be too extreme, confrontational and discomfiting to have any bearing on policy and practice in the UK where remarkable unanimity among all the key players continues to prevail over lifelong learning. But this more critical approach to lifelong learning may be more relevant to the UK than many of us think, particularly given the recent writings of Alan Tuckett[5], Director of the National Institute for Adult Continuing Education and Vice-Chair of the government's National Advisory Group for Continuing Education and Lifelong Learning:

> *I find to my surprise that I have been thinking about compulsory adult learning.... In the information industries continuing learning is a necessary precondition to keeping a job, and your capacity to keep on learning may affect the job security of others. Learning is becoming compulsory. And if it is true for people in some sectors of industry, why not for people who might want to rejoin the labour force later? (1998)*

It is not too difficult to detect in the above not only the voice of moral authoritarianism which Walter Heinz believes to be the hidden agenda behind the rhetoric, but also mounting frustration among liberal educators who, after 20 years in the political wilderness, have now become policy advisers, faced with the same, seemingly intractable statistics on low levels of participation in learning and training. But within a year, genuine social concern to widen the social base of participation is turning into threats of compulsion. How long before we see the official advertising slogan: 'You *will* learn and, what's more, you *will* enjoy it'?

In sum, the challenge of the emerging fourth model is to confront the argument that, behind the benevolent intentions and the high flown rhetoric, lifelong learning, the learning society and the learning organisation are all being propounded to induce individuals to become more-or-less willing participants in learning for life and to bear an increasing proportion of the costs of such learning without end. In the sense that society always employs a variety of social processes to ensure that its members conform to its changing expectations, lifelong learning is viewed by the proponents of the fourth model as the latest form of social control. The real value of this approach is that it breaks the cosy consensus on lifelong learning in the UK and may even provoke some much needed controversy and debate on the topic.

Notes

[1] The first publication in the series produced by The Policy Press contains articles by Michael Eraut et al (on learning from other people at work), David Ashton (on learning in organisations), Peter Scott and Antje Cockrill (on training in the construction industry in Wales and Germany), Reiner Siebert (on Jobrotation), Kari Hadjivassiliou et al (on continuous vocational training), and Stephen Baron et al (on what *The Learning Society* means for adults with learning difficulties).

[2] The first eight projects to complete will each produce an overview of their research in an edited collection of articles to be published by The Policy Press in the summer of 1999.

[3] David Raffe and his colleagues explain the use of the term 'home internationals' as follows: "The United Kingdom is represented at football by four 'national teams', those of England, Scotland, Wales and Northern Ireland, and matches between these teams were once called 'home internationals'" (Raffe et al, 1997, p 2). As each of these four 'countries' also has its own education and training system, the term 'home internationals' is used here to describe comparative research on these different systems.

[4] Witness, for example, the words of James Paice, the Minister for Training in John Major's government, "If we lack skills, we lose out. The economy, the performance of every business and the prosperity of every citizen suffer. We have no choice. We must all invest in learning for the future" (quoted by Nick Stuart in Coffield, 1997, p 67). Comparative research helps to dispel the economic determinism and the closure of debate on policy options which such arguments advocate.

[5] I am grateful to Kathryn Ecclestone for bringing this quotation to my attention.

References

Bernstein, B. (1996) *Pedagogy, symbolic control and identity*, London: Taylor and Francis.

Bynner, J. and Chisholm, L. (1998) 'Comparative youth transition research: methods, meanings and research relations', *European Sociological Review*, vol 14, no 2, pp 131-50.

Campaign for Learning Newsletter, 'I'd fancy some of that! Learning's better than sex', London: RSA, Issue 3, p 1.

Chisholm, L. (1987) 'Vorsprung ex machina? Aspects of curriculum and assessment in cultural comparison', *Journal of Educational Policy*, vol 2, no 2, pp 149-59.

Cohen, S. (1985) *Visions of social control*, Cambridge: Polity Press.

Coffield, F. (ed) (1997) *A national strategy for lifelong learning*, Department of Education, University of Newcastle.

CEC (Commission of the European Communities) (1997) *Towards a Europe of knowledge*, Luxembourg, COM (97) 563.

DfEE (Department for Education and Employment)/Cabinet Office (1996) *The skills audit: A report from an interdepartmental group*, London: DfEE/Cabinet Office.

DfEE (1998) *The Learning Age: A renaissance for a new Britain*, Cm 3790, London: The Stationery Office.

Dickens, C. (1952) *Our mutual friend*, Oxford: Oxford University Press.

European Commission (1995) *Teaching and learning: Towards the Learning Society*, White Paper on Education and Training, Luxembourg: Office for Official Publications of the EC.

Gipps, C. (1996) 'The paradox of Pacific Rim learners', *Times Educational Supplement*, 20 December.

Green, A. (1997) *Education, globalization and the nation state*, Houndmills: Macmillan.

Ignatieff, M. (1994) *Blood and belonging: Journeys into the new nationalism*, London: Vintage.

Jobert, A., Marry, C. and Tanguy, L. (1997) 'Comparisons between an area of research in Germany, Great Britain and Italy', in A. Jobert, C. Marry, L. Tanguy and H. Rainbird (eds) *Education and work in Great Britain, Germany and Italy*, London: Routledge.

Joseph Rowntree Foundation (1995) *Inquiry into Income and Wealth*, Joseph Rowntree Foundation: York.

Keep, E. (1991) 'The grass looked greener – some thoughts on the influence of comparative vocational training research on the UK policy debate', in P. Ryan (ed) *International comparisons of vocational education and training for intermediate skills*, London: Falmer Press, pp 23-46.

Kennedy, H. (1997) *Learning works: Widening participation in Further Education*, Coventry: Further Education Funding Council.

Lindholm, R. (1998) 'The Learning Age: towards a Europe of knowledge', Speech at DfEE International Conference on Lifelong Learning, Manchester, 18 May.

OST (Office of Science and Technology) (1995) *Progress through partnership: Leisure and learning*, London: HMSO.

Raffe, D. (1991) 'Scotland v England: the place of "home internationals" in comparative research', in P. Ryan (ed) *International comparisons of vocational education and training for intermediate skills*, London: Falmer Press, pp 47-67.

Raffe, D., Brannen, K., Croxford, L. and Martin, C. (1997) 'The case for home internationals in comparative research: comparing England, Scotland, Wales and Northern Ireland', Conference Paper, Dublin, September.

Reynolds, D. and Farrell, S. (1996) *Worlds apart? A review of international surveys of educational achievement involving England*, London: OFSTED.

Sargant, N., Field, J., Francis, H., Schuller, T. and Tuckett, A. (1997) *The learning divide*, Leicester: NIACE.

Temple, B. (1997) 'Watch your tongue: issues in translation and cross-cultural research', *Sociology*, vol 31, no 3, pp 607-18.

Tuckett, A. (1998) 'Recruits conscripted for the active age', *Times Educational Supplement*, 22 May.

Lifelong learning: learning for life? Some cross-national observations

Walter Heinz

Introduction

1996 was the 'year of lifelong learning', proclaimed by the European Commission. It said 'good-bye' without having been recognised by most employees and employers. What do we learn from that? Like the 'year of the child' and the 'year of the woman' it raises an important social issue and attempts to raise the profile of the topic in the minds of the public and of politicians. The year of lifelong learning was also characterised by quite different developments in unemployment in Europe. Great Britain managed to reduce the unemployment rate, while it keeps growing in Germany – of course with great variations between regions and industries. In both countries one (if not *the*) solution to not only the unemployment problem but also to improving the competitive edge in the global market is seen in expanding the concept of lifelong learning. However, as we will see, the definitions of lifelong learning and strategies linked to it differ substantially. The main issue seems to be the relative importance, combination, and sequence of general education, basic occupational education and training, specialised on-the-job training, and adult education.

On the agenda of policy makers and employers alike is the need to respond to changing job requirements and changing occupations by supplying the firm – nowadays called a 'learning organisation' – with highly flexible workers whose obligation it is to adapt themselves to the constant flux of skill demands and employment standards. But, if we can trust self-reports, only a third of employees in West Germany said in a survey that they experienced drastic occupational changes (Bolder et al, 1993; 1995). It depends largely on whether they define necessary adaptations to new technologies and forms of work organisation as modifications of skills or as a change in their job or profession.

Despite the rhetoric about technology-induced transformations of the workplace and impending change of careers, the majority of employees at least in West Germany feel that they can adapt to technological and organisational changes. Employers, however, are lobbying for an improvement to the links between initial vocational and Further Education (FE); its most important instrument is called 'promotional FE' (*Aufstiegsfortbildung*). This concept is strongly supported by the employers' associations which tell their members that human resource management has to signal that advancement depends not so much on certificates but on occupational involvement and achievement. Nevertheless, credentials and formalised certification are more important than ever for applicants to gain admittance to internal labour markets – in order to become a human resource which can then be managed.

In the German version, lifelong learning primarily means further occupational education which is seen as essential for coping with economic and technological changes. Stock-pile learning becomes less important than the link between basic and recurrent learning (BMBWFT, 1996). What used to be called 'adult education' is now a diffuse combination of self-organised learning and company-directed FE, in addition to retraining programmes for long-term unemployed people

(Friebel et al, 1993). In adult pedagogics the shift to lifelong learning and FE was criticised in the 1980s; lifelong learners were seen as 'victims of the qualification offensive'. However, in response to the anticipation of the effects of globalisation on the economy, we can now observe a paradigm shift in educational philosophy. Future-oriented adult education is supposed to receive its critical impulse from initial vocational and company-directed FE (Diepold, 1996). This shift from well-reasoned educational scepticism to organisational optimism goes hand in hand with the creation of a new mythical collective actor: 'the learning organisation'.

This perspective differs from the major English-speaking market societies. Because of the lack of an organised and publicly regulated system of initial vocational education, the UK, the USA and Canada tend to regard the usual sequences of short-term on-the-job training as the core of useful lifelong learning. There the debate about basic vocational education, training and FE has arisen only recently because the new information and communication technologies require a more developed skill and knowledge base. Britain has responded to these requirements by incorporating Further Education Colleges and by developing National Vocational Qualifications (NVQs). North America has a longer experience with non-university post-secondary institutions, the community colleges, but there is no vocational certification system.

Such institutions do not exist in Germany, which relies on a dual system of Vocational Education and Training (VET). And this system tends to produce not only more skills than are actually used at the workplace (ie, a skills surplus), *but also* the ability to get involved in institutionalised and self-organised lifelong learning.

In Germany, lifelong learning is contested terrain between employers, unions, FE providers, and the state (Bardeleben et al, 1996). It can be divided into three main segments: (1) company-directed FE; (2) public and self-organised learning; and (3) retraining programmes based on the federal job-creation law. Only some large companies conceive of lifelong learning as an anticipatory, planned investment in their labour force; most organise FE as a response to deficits in qualification. Therefore, company-based

FE rarely results in an 'educational surplus' for the employees. As in the UK, most of the small and medium-sized enterprises (SMEs) prefer short-term adjustments to technological innovations by introductory courses or on-the-job upgrading.

The widespread discrepancy between the rhetoric of lifelong learning and the reluctance of employers to invest in FE for all of their employees puts pressure on the workers to invest time and money privately in order to acquire the competence that they assume to be sufficient at least to keep their jobs (Geissler and Orthey, 1996).

Thus, the question must be raised: are companies really becoming 'investors' in people, does human resource development mean spending money on recurrent employee training and also contributing to the training of youth? No! The concentration on the concepts 'further education' and 'the learning organisation' seems to result in youth training and the retraining of the unemployed being handed over to private solutions in the family, the community, and the state. At least for the UK and North America the slogan 'let them eat skills' is changing to 'let them buy skills' with their own money. When lifelong learning, in whatever form, becomes a personal responsibility, the continuity and the repair of careers will require 'learning for life'. This metaphor is an expression of the modern trend to turn lifelong learning into a moral obligation and in many cases an external constraint. This mix of obligation and constraint rests on the assumption that skills and knowledge are already outdated when people have managed to learn them. This is the learning dimension which goes hand in hand with the trend of company restructuring and workplace reorganisation.

Lifelong learning compared

In the UK and North America lifelong learning is a substitute for initial VET and post-secondary education. However, there is also another version of lifelong learning: a way of life for academics and professionals who are members of professional organisations and who collect and read their journals and meet each other at conferences (David Lodge's 'small world').

In its social policy version, lifelong learning is a government-sponsored route for problem groups in the labour market. In this form it is a combination of compensating for gaps in basic education and making people employable who have fallen out of career paths or who were not given the opportunity to enter the labour market in the first place. Company-directed FE has as its primary goal the repair of skill deficits on demand, reflecting the just-in-time thinking of management. Expressed in a more friendly way, company-centred FE is organised to adapt the workforce to changing knowledge requirements and to prepare them for working in collaborative job arrangements. This also means delegating the responsibility for the work process and quality control to the workers.

Behind these manifest functions there is the hidden agenda of lifelong learning. It becomes a normative expectation to participate in recurrent, additional, or sequential learning whenever the internal or external job market calls for adjustments: 'education for life'. Furthermore, it socialises people to become more flexible or more employable without promising them job security.

Occupational Further Education in Germany

In 1994, 42% of all Germans aged 19 to 64 participated in *some kind* of FE; in 1979 the percentage was only 23%. *Occupational FE* increased between 1991 and 1994 from 21% to 24% (BMBWFT, 1996). These are rather moderate participation rates considering the rhetoric of lifelong learning. And there are differences between the new and old German states. Participation in retraining and other programmes is much more frequent in East Germany, which indicates higher unemployment rates.

In general, there is the well-known positive correlation between educational achievement, occupational status, and participation in FE. Employees with a post-secondary degree participate four times more frequently in occupational FE than employees without a vocational certificate. Only 4% report experiences of learning in quality circles or workshops; this contrasts strongly with the highly publicised movement of the 'learning organisation'.

Almost 700,000 people in the west and east of Germany are participants in retraining programmes that are organised in the framework of the job-promotion law. Some of the programmes are supported by the European Social Fund for long-term jobless, youths and women returners to the labour market.

Company-directed FE is discussed and promoted with the agenda of turning firms into learning organisations. This modernisation is accompanied by cost-cutting measures such as the outsourcing of FE, decentralised learning and job-based training. Big companies are shifting their education programs from providing to buying FE. The focus on the internal labour market and on the idea of the learning organisation corresponds to the fact that quite a number of companies now spend more on FE than on initial VET. This is a threat to the dual system. However, there is also a positive effect in the feedback of FE experiences for the reform of initial VET. In Germany, the current debate emphasises the development of broad occupational competence. "Modern FE has to include competence in problem-solving methods, abstract thinking, and social skills, in addition to specific occupational skills" (BMBWFT, 1996).

As in Britain and North America, FE in 'big companies' in Germany has the option to move from personnel administration and management to external services, from profit-centres to outsourcing. Internal FE operates as a quasi-enterprise by offering services to the companies' departments and divisions. As long as cost-cutting dominates, short-term qualification deficits will be repaired by offering adjustment packages. This, however, neglects the creation of qualification potentials that contain options for innovations in a 'bottom-up' direction which would be necessary to implement the learning organisation. The terminology used to describe this line of innovation in companies is quite revealing: from competence-centred to cost-centred to profit-centred FE. Obviously, the big company profits from a flexible crew of permanent or continuing learners by extending the just-in-time logic to the learning sequences for the modern employee. Finally, outsourcing facilitates the externalisation of FE to an independent firm. This is not primarily driven by the intention to improve the qualification of the entire labour force but by economic reasons to reduce costs and to increase effectiveness by buying custom-tailored FE. This is obviously a strategy for big companies, but SMEs do not have this option and depend on traditional external suppliers of FE (Friebel et al, 1993).

Another dimension has been recently added to the discourse of lifelong learning: the rediscovery of learning by acquiring knowledge through the labour process itself. The new forms of work organisation promise to turn FE back into the hands and minds of the employees by opening a wider range of options for designing work, collaboration, and quality control. Everyone becomes responsible for gearing their qualifications to the permanent improvement of the precarious balance of quality and efficiency. This strategy, however, is another aspect of learning for life because it increases the intensity of work and contributes to an intensification of short-term learning cycles.

Further education can also lead to the development and definition of new occupations. In the UK, NVQs have to be based on the creation of new occupational profiles, whereas in Germany there is both a tradition and a high level of public regulation concerning the links between initial VET and FE occupations. Though some new occupations start at the local and branch levels, they get formalised, first by a regional, and then finally by a federal, process of certification and standardisation. The German system is becoming more flexible to the extent that FE initiatives signal that existing VET curricula need to be reformed and may be combined to respond to new 'hybrid occupations'. Especially at the level of semi-professions and occupationally trained management positions, there is an increase of so-called interface qualifications, for instance 'office-marketing-technical' skill profiles that have led to the creation of new occupations like 'energy advisor', 'environmental specialist', 'manager of financial services', 'industrial master technician', or 'administrative assistant'.

Other countries like Canada have developed a different path. Canada has one of the highest post-secondary enrolments of all OECD countries (45%). Lifelong learning started in Canada as adult education which has become more and more vocationalised (Panu, 1988). After the Second World War, the former social policy orientation of adult education, which was seeking social transformation, disappeared. The growth of community colleges created a professionalised version of adult education in Canada. The main task was to produce salaried technicians, service, and semi-professional employees; the context was the ideology of the individual learner without an understanding of the potential social purpose of lifelong learning. Today, community colleges focus on vocational training and career education and have opened up the possibility of some post-secondary training to part-time students. Up to the 1970s, personal development, cultural studies, and general interest learning opportunities were available alongside occupational programmes, whereas today, adult education increasingly either serves the preparation of semi-professionals or the reintegration of the unemployed, mainly young people.

Obsolete education – outdated knowledge?

I would now like to turn to the question: who is the subject of lifelong learning? Information and communication technology and organisational restructuring do not necessarily lead to the end of work. Under optimal circumstances they could reduce the time spent at work and increase the time for education, social and political participation. Furthermore, a convergence of interest among employees in personal development with the requirements at the workplace for social and organisational skills might come about. The director of the Volkswagen division for education and training is enthusiastic about this potential convergence and is predicting a shift from skills training to general education.

For most employers, this brave new world will not enlarge autonomous learning. An opaque labour market requires substantial efforts in occupational self-management as a substitute for missing links between general education, occupational or professional education and career paths. In his classic study, *The great training robbery*, Ivar Berg (1970) documented for the USA that the critical determinants of work performance are not increased educational attainments but personal characteristics and job conditions. He criticised the mechanistic interpretation of the relationship between education and employment and the belief that it is individuals' educational achievements that decide what kind of job they get. Educational credentials are used primarily as screening devices by employers.

This seems to be a fair description of the current situation that creates demands for higher entrance qualifications and at the same time devalues these qualifications as not being sufficient because people's knowledge bases are declared to be outdated as soon as they have been awarded. In countries where careers are not organised through occupations and labour-market regulations but are shaped by personnel-management strategies, lifelong learning becomes mandatory, and employees become the company's 'social software'.

Please do not misunderstand my argument. I agree with Karl Marx's theory and the work of Melvin Kohn and Wolfgang Lempert that there is a close interrelationship between work activities, skill demands and personality development. Job enlargement and working in teams do increase the scope of activity and decision making which correlates with positive self-assessment and a collaborative attitude at work. In addition, opportunities for lifelong learning can indeed have positive effects on the animation of personal development and personal well-being as well as social participation.

Unfortunately, we do not know very much about the way employees themselves assess the options and constraints of lifelong learning. How can we explain the fact that not even half of the employed population in Germany has participated in any kind of FE? As a multilevel study (Bolder et al, 1993 and 1995) with a representative sample has documented recently, the likelihood of participating in employment-related FE declines with low educational and occupational status; with the exception, of course, of programmes for the long-term unemployed. There are big differences between men and women: men are more often involved in firm-based FE, women in public (*Volkshochschule*) or self-organised settings. Furthermore, participation in self-organised learning, regardless of gender, varies between 3% among unskilled workers and 60% for higher civil servants, and self-employed people.

Looking at the reasons for participation, this study found that the dominant personal goal is the actualisation and extension of job-related occupational knowledge. It seems that occupational FE is not seen by employees primarily as a means of achieving promotion but as a way to adapt to changing management demands and job requirements. This motivation corresponds to the statements of the *non*-participants; two thirds of them said that occupational FE will not lead to improvements in the content and conditions of their work. And the second important reason for *not* participating was fear of additional stress.

Thus, we can conclude that conditions at work and position in the occupational hierarchy are important in making decisions about participating or not participating in company-based FE. It is the organisational circumstances that transform general economic trends and public programmes into certain individual patterns of accepting or abstaining from lifelong learning. However, the personal circumstances, work experiences, family obligations, and life goals and, typical for Germany, the specific occupational culture, also influence the form and intensity of lifelong learning.

Further Education and social inequality

Turning or returning to any form of learning after a period of formal education has a different meaning for higher-level occupations where self-organised learning is taken for granted, and lower-level and disadvantaged employees and the jobless. For the growing number of mostly young and female non-standard workers and jobseekers, the participation in formal and informal lifelong learning is an attempt to compensate individuals for class differentials in initial educational attainment. Seen from this perspective, occupational FE and retraining operate as instruments of social selection. As Jonsson et al (1996) have recently concluded from a comparative study of educational attainment in Sweden, the UK and Germany: "The association with social background and educational attainment in a given country, for a given point in time, is produced both by circumstances relating to the family of origin and by the institutional characteristics of the educational system" (p 202). In the last decade in Germany, increasingly higher levels of initial education were required to enter an apprenticeship in white-collar occupations. This has caused working-class families to send their children to middle-level or higher-level secondary schools. Attaining such an education, furthermore, opened up greater opportunities to continue education at post-secondary levels and to combine initial vocational training with more advanced and continuing education that may contribute to an improvement of career options. If we look at performance-related attainment in the education system, there is little evidence of an equalisation in Britain. The association between class origin and educational attainment is not only a result of different performance levels (grades), but of choices concerning vocational and academic pathways following the completion of secondary school. Further Education colleges in the UK may provide the opportunity for individuals to equalise social class differences in the distribution of educational attainment, just by keeping young people occupied with the acquisition of basic and employment-related skill profiles. It is doubtful, however, whether this learning arrangement can contribute to the attenuation of social inequality in a generation that will be confronted with fundamental deregulations of the labour market. The rising importance of personal and social qualifications as recruitment criteria tends to turn the participation in FE into a criterion of willingness to engage in lifelong learning – as an indicator of enterprising and not just employable personalities.

As Brown and Scase (1994) argue in their book *Higher education and corporate realities*, an anti-industrial or anti-vocational bias characterises higher education and may be also the culture of FE in England. The initial and post-secondary education systems are not providing advancement channels for those who do not acquire the graduation symbols for 'fast-track careers'. They are referred to FE as part of the sequence of lifelong learning instead of continuing formal post-secondary education. Furthermore, the reason for establishing Training and Enterprise Councils (TECs) to manage initial and further vocational education is the reluctance of employers to provide transferable skills. This contrasts with the German tradition of providing occupational career options and access to FE which

are based on the completion of firm-based VET. In the less regulated labour markets of Great Britain and North America, the training and FE strategies of employers are limited because of their fear of poaching.

The consequence of such strategies is enforcing a 'customer-contract model' on VET and FE that only superficially contributes to the empowerment of the holders of Youth Credits or Career Development Loans. As David Atkinson (1996) summarised in his report on the English system: "We have reached the situation of VET being a commodity to be bought and sold without reference to anything but supply and demand".

Pitfalls of comparative analysis

Shavit and Blossfeld (1993) conclude from a large comparative project that class inequalities in educational attainment remain persistent over time. Jonsson et al (1996) find the opposite when comparing the UK, Sweden and Germany. They argue that weaknesses in databases and differences in conceptualising social origin may conceal trends toward decreasing social inequality. Some studies have been using prestige or socioeconomic scales in order to measure and to compare social origin; others tend to use social class indicators. Very rarely is comparative research based on a careful analysis of the institutional frameworks that regulate labour markets and organise general education, vocational education and training, FE and academic post-secondary education. Educational attainment has different implications for social inequality and the options and requirements of lifelong learning when school-based, firm-based, and mixed systems dominate in different countries. The 'CASMIN' project (Comparative Analysis of Mobility in Industrial Nations, by Erikson and Goldthorpe, 1992) – which, however, has not covered birth cohorts from the 1950s and later that experienced extensive structural changes of the education and labour-market structure – has documented that it is even more difficult to make comparable codings for educational attainment and the variety of lifelong learning arrangements than achieving comparable codings of class origin (see Erikson and Jonsson, 1996). For instance, there is one code for comparing the USA, Sweden and Great Britain that merges higher vocational and technical education and another code that combines compulsory and some vocational education. In the three countries these two codes hide a variety of different combinations of school-based, firm-based, or social policy-driven programmes and, what is even more serious, the relative value of vocational and academic attainments, as a major reflection of the distribution of life chances and cultural standards, vanishes by lumping the different education patterns together. Therefore, it gets extremely difficult to develop sound explanations for contrasting observations. On the one hand, the proportion of a birth cohort accomplishing significant and higher-level educational mile-stones is increasing; on the other hand, class differences in educational attainment still exist. To solve such a problem, the different forms of formal and informal lifelong learning and the differential rates of participation and non-participation have to be studied on three levels:

- the institutional fabric of the education system and the provisions for school-to-work and employment transitions (the problem of transparency and permeability), as well as the occupational structure;

- the cultural traditions that tend to legitimise the unequal distribution of general education and post-secondary attainment (the tension between academism and vocationalism); and last, but not least

- the personal living circumstances and strategies of adjustment, withdrawal and protest concerning the requirement for lifelong learning.

One promising approach to comparing the relationships between educational attainment, employment and careers is to focus on occupations by matching respondents in different countries by skill profiles (see Evans and Heinz, 1994).

Lifelong learning: different paths but comparable standards?

The main goal of FE programmes and initiatives in the European Union (eg, the Leonardo Programme) is to improve equal opportunities in the FE system and to promote cooperation between the social partners. In this respect, quality control is not

enough. Certifying FE arrangements in the framework of quality management (DIN/ISO9000) tends to be motivated by corporate identity, marketing reasons and by a preventive defence against state regulations. They thus become symbolic politics. Without defining learning rights across the life-course, that also promote individual reflection of social relationships, of individual and collective interests, lifelong learning initiatives and programmes will have difficulties in attenuating the social inequalities of life chances. It will be necessary to check the commercialisation of lifelong learning by reducing the increasing externalisation of FE by companies. Instead of having to 'buy skills' in order to keep abreast with the changing work requirements and employment standards, continuing education should support individuals to find out about alternatives at life-course transitions and turning points. This approach would call for a combined system of vocational and FE counselling which regards lifelong learning not only as a way for increasing human capital but also as a means to participate in social, cultural and political affairs.

It is a policy choice to separate or integrate education and work. Education can further the ability to understand and solve problems inside and outside the world of work if we ask what the uses of knowledge are instead of talking about the management of knowledge. Without good schools and public responsibility for their quality and their contribution to equality, people may learn something, but not how to relate options for lifelong learning to their life course.

References

Atkinson, D. (1996) 'Financial and fiscal arrangements for stimulating participation in vocational education and training – a case of the UK', in Netherlands Economic Institute (ed) *Incentives for participation in vocational education and training*, Rotterdam.

Bardeleben, R.V., Bolder, A. and Heid, A. (eds) (1996) *Kosten und Nutzen der beruflichen Bildung* (Beiheft 12 zur Zeitschrift für Berufs- und Wirtschaftspädagogik), Stuttgart: Steiner.

Berg, I. (1970) *Education and jobs: The great training robbery*, New York: Praeger.

Bolder, A. et al (1993 and 1995) *Weiterbildungsabstinenz*, 2 vols (Berichte des ISO), Köln.

Brown, P. and Scase, R. (1994) *Higher education and corporate realities*, London: UCL Press.

BMBWFT (Bundesminsterium für Bildung, Wissenschaft, Forschung und Technologie) (1996) *Berufsbildungsbericht 1996*, Bonn: BMBWFT.

Diepold, P. (ed) (1996) *Berufliche Aus- und Weiterbildung* (BeitrAB 195), Nürnberg: IAB.

Erikson, R. and Goldthorpe, J.H. (1992) *The constant flux: A study of class mobility in industrial societies*, Oxford: Oxford University Press.

Erikson, R. and Jonsson, J.O. (eds) (1996) *Can education be equalised? The Swedish case in comparative perspective*, Bolder, CO: Westview Press.

Evans, K. and Heinz, W.R. (eds) (1994) *Becoming adults in England and Germany*, London: Anglo-German Foundation.

Friebel, A. et al (1993) *Weiterbildungsmarkt und Lebenszusammenhang*, Bad Heilbrunn.

Geissler, K. and Orthey, F.M. (1996) 'Die Ungleichheit der Subjekte und die Gleichheit der Zumutungen. Erwachsenenbildung als Einheit von Differenzen', in A. Bolder, W.R. Heinz and K. Rodax (eds) *Die Wiederentdeckung der Ungleichheit* (Jahrbuch 'Bildung und Arbeit'), Opladen: Leske & Budrich.

Jonsson, J.O., Mills, C. and Müller, W. (1996) 'A half century of increasing educational openness? Social class, gender, and educational attainment in Sweden, Germany, and Britain', in R. Erikson and J.O. Jonsson (eds) *Can education be equalised? The Swedish case in comparative perspective*, Boulder, CO: Westview Press.

Panu, R.S. (1988) 'Adult education, economy, and state in Canada', *The Alberta Journal of Educational Research*, vol 34, pp 232-45.

Shavit, Y. and Blossfeld, H.P. (eds) (1993) *Persistent inequality: Changing educational attainment in thirteen countries*, Boulder, CO: Westview Press

2

Models of guidance services in the learning society: the case of the Netherlands

Teresa Rees and Will Bartlett

Introduction

A central feature of *fin de siècle* postwar capitalism is the increasing awareness of uncertainty, risk and insecurity. Despite an almost unprecedented world-wide boom which seems to defy conventional concepts of the business cycle, mass consumer demand is constrained by a widespread fear of unemployment. Labour markets have become more turbulent and flexible, and labour contracts have become increasingly fixed-term or part-time (Hutton, 1995). In many areas of industry, old concepts of a job for life and of a long-term psychological contract between employer and employee have begun to break down (Collin and Watts, 1996). Labour market participants increasingly expect to make frequent job changes and indeed occupational changes in the course of their working lives (Commission on Social Justice/ IPPR, 1994). In the new service industries, the need for flexibility and adaptability to ever-changing consumer fashions creates an in-built impermanence of employment in the most dynamic sector of modern economies. The greatest share of new job creation in the most advanced economies is accounted for in the growing sector of small and medium-sized businesses, but these jobs disappear almost as rapidly as they are created since the bulk of small businesses collapse before they reach maturity (Storey, 1994). At the same time, rapid technological change is creating a demand for an ever more highly skilled labour force. Alongside changing jobs, individuals are faced with the need to develop new skills, to retrain and to periodically re-engage with the institutions of formal education.

These shifts, spurred on by technological change and increased global competition, have stimulated interest in, and debate upon, the concept of a learning society. It is argued in many quarters that the key to success in the modern hyper-competitive global economy is the development of the skills of the labour force (Commission on Public Policy and British Business, 1997; Reich, 1992). The competitive advantage of nations is no longer to be found solely in the accumulation of either physical or financial capital which is globally mobile, but in the accumulation of skills and knowledge which have become the new scarce resource.

Even these are not enough. With rapid technological change it is the ability to re-skill and re-train the labour force which is held to distinguish the more successful economies from the less successful. We call this approach *the skill-growth model* of the learning society. However, there are a variety of other views of what a learning society should be or aim to achieve. Some commentators are sceptical of an overly simplistic and deterministic link between improvements in skills and the achievement of more rapid economic growth. Instead they point to the need for a more voluntarist approach in which the aim of the learning society should be an increase in capacities to achieve individual self-fulfilment in all spheres of life, not just in economic activities. This approach highlights a concern for equity in order to supplement the search for greater efficiency emphasised by those who focus on the link between skill formation and economic growth (Keep and Mayhew, 1996). We refer to this second approach as *the personal development model* of the learning society.

There is also a third view, which to some extent addresses both concerns, and which emphasises the role of institutions of trust and cooperation in promoting economic growth on an equitable basis. In this view it is not human capital (training, education) but rather social capital (networks, communications and the strength of civil society) which is the binding constraint to the effective deployment of accumulated capital, skills and other resources in pursuit of economic growth (Putnam, 1993a; 1993b; Fukuyama, 1995). However, such social capital can only be developed through a process of *social learning* (Wilson, 1997), a process which offers a more participative and community-based approach to the development of a learning society.

Whatever one's view concerning the form which a learning society should take, its effectiveness is likely to depend significantly upon individuals being able to make informed choices about employment, education and training opportunities on a continual basis. If lifelong learning is to become a reality, accessible ports of entry and routes of progression will be needed in education and training systems. Individuals are increasingly expected to create their own trajectories between education, training, employment, unemployment and non-employment, combining learning activities with different employment statuses. Career guidance services, traditionally oriented towards helping school leavers manage the transition from education to working life, will be increasingly needed to provide information, advice, counselling and other forms of support to adults as they traverse a flexible career path between a variety of jobs and between a variety of economic and social roles. Education guidance, too, will need to play an increasing role in assisting individual choice between the growing variety of education and training opportunities and opportunity providers.

However, different approaches to the form that a learning society should take carry different implications for the appropriate mode of delivery and structure of operation of guidance services. In *the skill-growth model*, the role of guidance services is to provide a brokerage service for adults seeking a suitable niche in the labour market, in education and in training. Such services can be described as seeking to facilitate the smooth operation of the labour market and the associated emerging learning market. In *the personal development model*, this role of job-matching and provision of access to formal education and training opportunities is played down. Rather, guidance is needed at all points on a career path, not just at points of transition. This underpins ideas of guidance for employed people in addition to new entrants (and returners) to the labour market, education and training. The approach is consistent with innovative measures such as the Ford EDAP scheme, which gives employees opportunities for personal development training in addition to conventional occupational training. In *the social learning model*, the role of the guidance worker is one of facilitator of social action rather than one of simple job matching or of guiding personal development on an individualised basis. Guidance is integrated with social action and is consistent with the growth of third sector providers (eg, social cooperatives, voluntary organisations) which interact with users, not only to improve their access to the job and education market, but also to facilitate a social learning process and promote community development. Of course, these various approaches are not necessarily mutually exclusive and may operate alongside each other in a complementary way.

In the project we report on here, we consider the changing forms of guidance in a number of different European countries and interpret their significance in the light of the various models of the learning society which we have outlined above[1]. A wide variety of approaches to the provision of guidance services is evident throughout the European Union (EU) countries (Watts et al, 1993). These range from the marketised systems of the Netherlands and the UK to the centralised state-managed systems found in Germany, through the pluralistic model found in France to the more decentralised system based largely on non-profit providers found in Italy. In most countries there is a mix of various modes of provision, but the mix varies from one country to another. Hence, in some countries state provision is important but in others such as France and the UK (for school leavers), quasi-market forms of provision can be found in which services remain publicly funded but are delivered on a competitive basis by a range of independent public, private or third sector providers. In this case, services are provided to users without charge at the point of delivery. The purpose of a quasi-market of this type is to induce synthetic market competition between providers of public services in the hope that this will improve the efficiency with which services are delivered to the public (Le Grand and Bartlett, 1993). Elsewhere there is a trend, more marked in the Netherlands and UK (for adults) than in France or Germany, towards the full marketisation of guidance services – making a market of the market brokers (Watts, 1995). In such cases a genuine market has been developed in which users pay for services, although there may be an element of public subsidy involved in order to stimulate demand. In the case of the UK, combinations of both these methods have been implemented at different stages of the guidance process, with free information combined with user fees for more in-depth guidance services (eg, individual counselling, group sessions, psychometric testing).

Our approach to comparative research has involved working in close collaboration with research partners in the four countries selected for the study: France, Germany, Italy and the Netherlands. The countries were selected for the research on the basis of a reading of the existing literature on the subject, in particular a cross-national study compiled by the EC. This provided us with an initial typology of the organisation of guidance services across Europe, ranging from the centralised approach adopted in Germany to the highly decentralised approach adopted in Italy, with intermediate approaches adopted in the other two countries. We were interested in exploring this variation and comparing the different approaches adopted elsewhere in Europe to the systems set up by the Conservative government in its reforms to the local authority careers services initiated in 1994.

We began the research by initially selecting four research partners, one in each of the countries concerned. We did this by taking advice from experts in the field and through our previous contacts in various European research projects in which we had been previously engaged. This resulted in our identifying four highly expert and interested research partners with whom we have worked closely throughout the study.

The approach we adopted was to break down the research task into a number of discrete stages. In the

first we contacted the research partners with our proposals and an outline of the study. We requested them to prepare a series of background papers for us, setting out the basics of the way guidance services were organised in their countries. On the basis of these background papers we agreed with our research partners on a programme of interviews with officials and key informants at the various organisations involved in the provision of guidance services in the respective countries.

The field research itself took place through a series of short visits, one to each country, by the UK researchers. Our research partners organised an interview schedule and all interviews were made by combined teams of the UK researchers and the research partners in each country. Interviews were therefore conducted by both ourselves and our foreign partners working closely together, with periods in between interviews used for writing up notes and for intensive discussions of the key points to emerge from each interview. At the end of each field trip there would be a meeting to reflect upon and draw out the main findings and an outline for a country report to be written up jointly by the UK researchers and the foreign partners as a first draft. These research reports were then presented at an international seminar involving the entire research group and a set of invited experts which was held at the University of Bristol in September 1997. The research reports were then revised in the light of comments received at the seminar, in preparation for full publication either as separate research papers or as part of the book which will be published as an output of the project.

The main advantages of this method of working have been the close collaboration of the UK and the foreign research partners. The research topic inevitably involved a deep understanding of the distinctive institutional environment and context in four different European countries. It was unlikely that the UK researchers would have been able to gain a deep insight into this institutional background without the assistance of the research partners, most of whom had already been engaged in the research on the topic in their own countries. By working closely and 'jointly' with the research partners, however, the UK researchers were able to guide and influence the choice of interviewees and to ensure that the field research was carried out within a common analytical framework. An additional advantage has been the creation of a European-wide network of researchers who are in a position to carry forward research on this and related themes after the conclusion of the ESRC project.

This paper examines the changing nature of funding and delivery of adult guidance services within one particular Member State, the Netherlands, within the framework of these contrasted models of the learning society. However, all Member States of the EU are to an extent influenced by their location within the Single Market, the policies of the EU in promoting economic competitiveness and avoiding social exclusion, and by the availability of EU funding for guidance activities. Before examining adult guidance services in the Netherlands, therefore, the next section briefly reviews these contextual factors. The concluding section assesses the extent to which changes in the systems of provision of guidance services are consistent with one or other (or indeed any) of the three approaches to the learning society which we have developed above.

The EU context

The Single Market

The removal of restrictions on the mobility of labour within the EU as a result of the creation of the Single Market in 1992 had considerable implications, in theory at least, for the spatial dimension of information and advice which guidance services are now called upon to provide (Banks et al, 1990; Watts, 1995). While the extent of human mobility may be rather less developed than anticipated in some quarters (see Field, 1997), nevertheless, jobseekers are technically able to choose between vacancies anywhere within the EU. Hence there is an onus of responsibility upon those working in locally-based employment services to make available information about opportunities on an EU-wide basis, and not just for employment but for education and training opportunities.

Methods of tackling this are being explored by EURES, the European network of employment services and other institutions interested in labour mobility, including the European Commission (EC) itself. There is also a core network of 400 trained advisers to deal specifically with the transnational jobseekers and job providers (EC, 1994b, pp 37/8).

One of the major developments in guidance services in recent years has been the computerisation of databases: this is particularly significant for storing information at the EU level. As part of the activities of EURES, both a computerised jobs databank and a living and working conditions databank are being set up (EC, 1994b). Many private companies are developing a market in this field, selling their databases and software to a range of bodies which include guidance among their activities.

Closer links between guidance professionals in higher education are being facilitated by FEDORA (*Fédération Européen de l'Orientation Académique*) and annual European conferences are now held on computers in careers guidance (Petan, 1994). Hence the net effect of the Single Market on guidance services in the Member States has been to encourage transnational cooperation between providers and to provide an additional imperative for the computerisation of information.

European policy

During the 1990s, the EC has produced three White Papers which, combined with the provisions of the Social Chapter and the agreements reached on the new Treaty at the June 1997 Amsterdam Summit, set the framework of policy making at the EU level well into the next millennium. The first White Paper was on economic policy, *Growth competitiveness employment: The challenges and ways forward into the 21st century* (EC, 1994a), the second on social policy, *European social policy: A way forward for the Union* (EC, 1994b) and the third on teaching and learning, *Teaching and learning: Towards the Learning Society* (EC, 1996).

The key element of these policy documents is a twin concern with fostering economic competitiveness and with the avoidance of 'social exclusion' (Rees, 1998). The notion of a learning society is a central plank in both these objectives. Improving the skills of the workforce through vocational education and training is identified as crucial to the development of the economic competitiveness of the Single Market (Rainbird, 1993). This fits the first of our models of the learning society: skills are identified as important for economic growth.

In the economic White Paper, active labour market policies are discussed in terms of creating a better match between labour supply and demand through developing closer liaisons with undertakings or by the establishment of private employment agencies. New, more labour intensive service activities are advocated which might suggest underpinning the second of our models of the learning society (personal development), but the discourse is couched very firmly in terms of 'encouraging people to work'. The Paper also discusses one of the major concerns of Member States, the cost of welfare, and advocates an examination of social protections systems to target benefits to those most in need (EC, 1994a, pp 140, 141).

Skill development is also seen as essential in the social policy White Paper, in order to maximise the opportunities of the socially excluded to gain paid work. While some of the discussion of social exclusion is somewhat closer to the second model of a learning society outlined in the introduction, geared towards personal development and self-fulfilment, it is couched in terms of an end result of enhancing human resources and reducing welfare costs. As Levitas observes, the socially excluded are defined in terms of their exclusion from the working labour force (Levitas, 1996). The role of EURES is described in the social policy White Paper as a "forum for discussion of European employment issues at the operational level", but this is exclusively in terms of its remit "to inform, counsel and place job-seekers" (EC, 1994a, p 37). This suggests a dominant model still geared very closely to guidance as a brokerage service.

The third White Paper is the one most focused on the development of a learning society: the *Teaching and learning* paper. Here again, the model of a learning society is one firmly linked to skills development. An appropriate guidance service is envisaged as one which promotes open access to information and guidance, servicing individual aptitudes and needs (EC, 1996, p 34). The observation is made that currently, the citizen of

Europe has more information available to assist the process of selecting of hotels and restaurants than learning opportunities (p 34). It is emphasised that we need to know how occupations will develop and what skills will be needed in the future at the European level. The White Paper appears to be based on the belief that better information about learning and job opportunities will automatically lead to the enhancement of skills and thus improve the economic efficiency of the labour market. However, it is also stated in the White Paper that "social origins continue to *condition choices* made by individuals which can work against their social advancement" (EC, 1996, p 35) (authors' emphasis). This concern about the influence of social attributes on choice indicates an acknowledgement of the social construction of learning and labour markets.

Individuals' choices are influenced to a greater or lesser extent by an awareness of the role of gender, race and other discriminators in the organisation of the labour market. The emphasis in Commission documentation on well-informed choices understates the effect of these factors. Nevertheless, the operation of social features in the allocation of positions in the labour market is acknowledged in that people with certain characteristics are identified as belonging to 'disadvantaged groups': these are then targeted in social policy. The causes of group disadvantage are not addressed.

The EU's position on guidance can therefore be described as having both economic efficiency and social equity objectives. The vision of the learning society underlying these policies appears to correspond to the skills-growth model, although there is some room for the personal development model, if only in order to deliver the first more effectively. Both these models rely on the creation of effective, formal guidance services to deliver their goals and this is reflected in the approach taken by the EC to funding guidance activities in the Member States.

EU as funder of guidance activities

EU support for guidance activities is closely linked to the funding of education, training and employment programmes and this has impacted upon the nature and provision of guidance services in the Member States. Through European Social

Fund (ESF) projects and Community Initiatives such as ADAPT and EMPLOYMENT, and through SOCRATES (the EC's action programme on education) and LEONARDO DA VINCI (the EC's action programme on training), a range of public, private and third sector organisations are accessing resources to support projects which include a guidance component. The growth of third sector providers is a particularly important feature of the EU approach since many of their activities are concerned with target groups identified as disadvantaged in the labour market.

The Community Initiatives ADAPT and EMPLOYMENT (with its targeted strands NOW, HORIZON and YOUTHSTART) include support for guidance described by the Commission in the following terms (EC, 1995, pp 10, 11):

ADAPT   Development and reinforcement of guidance and counselling services (within the framework of industrial restructuring).

NOW   (New Opportunities for Women) assistance for the creation or development of guidance/ counselling and training services for women.

HORIZON   Support for the creation of personalised counselling services and setting up reception/ guidance service centres for people who are handicapped and/or threatened with exclusion.

YOUTHSTART   Definition of objectives and standards in the field of vocational guidance for young people in difficulty.

A new strand in the EMPLOYMENT Community Initiative, INTEGRA, has since been introduced to target vulnerable and disadvantaged groups who find to difficult to find work: INTEGRA also includes a guidance component.

Projects and exchanges funded under SOCRATES, LEONARDO DA VINCI and EMPLOYMENT are transnational, allowing social partners, students and lecturers, trainers and trainees to visit and work with their partner organisations in other Member States. While the EC has put some emphasis on the need for guidance within these activities, it has not specified its nature or duration. The net effect is to provide some underpinning for guidance activities and to provide resources for a range of organisations involved in their delivery.

The influence of European funding has highlighted cultural differences in the conceptualisation of 'guidance' (see Rees et al, 1999: forthcoming). It is through the diversity of approaches to guidance activities, co-funded by the EU, that we can trace differences among and within Member States in the modelling of a learning society and in the treatment of 'disadvantaged groups'.

One illustration of the differences is provided through space created within programmes for projects which enhance the equal treatment of men and women. This is a principle which was enshrined in the 1957 Treaty of Rome. The legislation that underpinned it did little to remove the pay gap between men and women or to challenge the rigidities of patterns of gender segregation in education, training or the labour market. In recognition of this, in the 1980s the Commission introduced a series of positive action measures, in effect projects designed to bring women's skills up to the level of men (Rees, 1998). These measures have supported a range of third sector organisations offering training and guidance for women throughout the EU within a series of Action Programmes on Equal Treatment for Men and Women which include guidance activities.

More recently, the EU has extended its equal treatment approach to a range of other equality dimensions. In the Amsterdam summit, there was a commitment to extend the principle of equal treatment to people on the grounds of disability, ethnic origin and race, religious belief, sexual orientation and age. This endorses growing concerns about the 'social exclusion' of such groups, although the nature of their exclusion is not clearly articulated. However, the position of positive action measures for women is underlined in the new Treaty and mainstreaming equality is identified as the major policy approach to equality in the future, that is, integrating equal opportunities into all Community policies, programmes and actions. This contrasts with the approach of informed choice in the labour and learning markets supplemented by special treatment of disadvantaged groups which underpins the three White Papers.

EU policy towards developing a European approach to guidance services has to contend with, and work within a wide variety of different approaches taken towards guidance services in the various Member States. The UK and the Netherlands share a pattern of deregulation and marketisation of guidance services. Typically, providers compete for contracts to provide services. Public money is used to provide a public service but one which may be provided by a private sector supplier. As the providers need to compete successfully for such contracts, alternative sources of funding are eagerly sought. In this context, European funding has become an increasingly significant source of additional funding. On the other hand, in Italy, where there is little in the way of state provision or funding of guidance services, EU support is critical in promoting the activities of newly emerging third sector providers. In Germany, where the state sponsors a highly centralised network of guidance services, EU support has a far more marginal impact.

The next section explores recent changes in the nature of guidance services in one Member State, the Netherlands, to seek to demonstrate the way in which EU support interacts with and influences the direction of policy at a national level on the nature and pattern of guidance services delivered. The paper concludes with some comments about contrasting Member States where different models operate and where guidance services are shaped by other drivers.

Adult guidance services in the Netherlands

In the Netherlands, a programme of decentralisation and deregulation has characterised guidance services in recent years. In a major policy initiative in the context of declining public funding, the Departments of Education and Employment brought together their guidance activities into a more streamlined approach to provide a back-up service behind the front-line practitioners in schools (career teachers) and the Employment Service (placement officers). This has inevitably meant a

merging of quite different cultures and the setting up of second and third line support services. The Employment Service, which had traditionally employed its own psychologists for guidance work, was also decentralised. Local offices could buy in their services from the regional bureaux or from commercial providers. Similarly schools, which had been able to draw at will upon the services of the state subsidised regional bureaux, were given block grants from which they could pay for such services and state subsidies for the regional bureaux are being phased out. Schools are obliged by law to provide some guidance but the nature and extent of such guidance is not specified. The block grant funding revealed the true cost of guidance services which had been provided by state subsidised regional bureaux. As a result, many schools now prefer to rely on guidance teachers rather than buy in expertise from the regional bureaux. Similarly, some Employment Service offices could continue to employ their own psychologists or buy in services on the market.

To reduce the budget of the Employment Service, the registered unemployed were divided into four categories according to their 'distance' from the labour market. It was argued that those 'nearest' the labour market (ie, the most 'placeable') did not need the help of the Service. At the other end of the continuum, responsibility for those with difficulties such as drug addiction which impeded their realistic likelihood of placement, was shifted to the municipalities. The Employment Service were left with the two intermediary groups. Much of the emphasis in the approach is on training: the Employment Service has its own training schools to develop the employability of its clients.

As a consequence of these changes, some of the second line providers, the regional bureaux, are in financial trouble. Indeed, of the original 16, only 12 still survive. Some of those made redundant or fired have set up their own private companies and offer services to schools more cheaply. The regional bureaux increasingly look to European funding to supplement their income and use their contacts with schools to participate in projects which include some guidance work. In the Netherlands, newly privatised providers at local, regional and national level make considerable use of EU-funding for guidance activities.

Providers have been forced to reorient themselves with regard to the 'added-value' of guidance, and to sell themselves. Moreover, this creation of a market has led to the growth of independent providers seeking to sell guidance services to schools and other clients. Further Education Colleges now offer six-week courses in guidance which, the prospectuses say, enable graduates to apply for acceptance into one of the professional bodies. This appears to be a marketing ploy, however, as the professional bodies are reluctant to admit graduates from such courses. These professional bodies are in crisis and there are growing concerns about the quality of what is received in the schools which do not buy in services.

Guidance, as a result of deregulation, is now more integrated into other activities such as personal development, outplacement and continuing education and training. This has led to difficulties for traditional practitioners from both the Employment Service, who focus on job matching, and for guidance workers used to operating in school settings. Both have had to broaden their range and context. According to Meijers (1997), while deregulation adversely affected the old infrastructure and weakened power relations connected with guidance, it cleared the way for a new orientation of the entire field. This included a shift in the content of guidance (from testing and matching to career learning); changes with respect to organisational context (from an isolated activity to an integral part of the education or placement process); and new patterns of cooperation (from the 'xenophobia' of psychologists and career teachers to cooperation with human resource management and human resource development professionals).

The marketisation of guidance has led to the development and professionalisation of third level work in the form of the National Careers Guidance Information Centre which again runs on the basis of contracts. Originally its work focused on developing an information base on educational and occupational opportunities. Now it is more focused on developing theoretical frameworks and methodologies. The centre is involved in a considerable number of LEONARDO DA VINCI projects.

In the Netherlands there have been profound changes in the way that adult guidance services are organised and in the nature of guidance activities that are now supported. The emphasis has been on integration with other activities. The marketisation of guidance services has led to shifts away from client-centred guidance to more labour market orientated work albeit rooted within an educational curriculum, or within a back to work trajectory for the unemployed. Guidance for employees is on the increase, and some of those made redundant are offered the choice of a redundancy package or outplacement guidance by their employers. The marketisation of guidance and the need to find contracts has led to the Netherlands being one of the (proportionately) biggest contractants for European projects such as LEONARDO.

There has been some criticism of the client-centred nature of guidance work with Employment Service clients: it was not sufficiently related to the labour market. In this sense we see a shift in model from a concern with professional development to a skills-growth, employment-centred learning society.

Conclusion

As we argued in the introduction, differences in the underlying policy models of a learning society imply corresponding differences in the approaches taken to the development of careers and education guidance services. In the light of the preceding discussion we can begin to draw out a few of these linkages and in doing so gain a better understanding of the implications of and reasons for the variety of approaches towards guidance services in the EU.

In the rhetoric of the EC, we see a skill-growth model of the learning society underpinning economic, social and teaching and learning policies but with some space for special groups who need particular projects and guidance to steer them away from limiting choices. The range of special groups has been expanded from women to include a broad raft of equality dimensions. For such disadvantaged target groups, the personal development model of guidance is accommodated within funding allowed for positive action projects in order to combat exclusion, but with the ultimate aim of adding to the stock of human resources.

In the Netherlands, we saw a distinction being made between groups according to their distance from the labour market and the kinds of guidance activity allowable varying accordingly. Again the learning society model underpinning such an approach is a skill-growth model. Guidance is now integrated into learning activities and back-to-work trajectories. The commercial sector has developed rapidly in response to the marketisation of services and to funding opportunities available from the EU. We see here then two models in operation simultaneously.

Like the Netherlands, guidance services in Britain have also been marketised and careers companies now compete for contracts to provide services. Core contracts are for young people but government funding is also available for adult services for which careers companies compete. Again, European funding is regarded as essential to survival for many companies, despite the abundance of administrative work attached to it. Some companies are merging, there have been some hostile takeovers of neighbouring patches and there are some new entrants. There is some support for the integration of the Employment Service and the careers service companies because of the Labour government's New Deal policies. Both the Netherlands and the UK therefore come closest to the skill-growth model.

Among the growing number of third sector providers in Germany, and in our Scottish case study, where adult guidance is provided by the local authority under a combined social and economic regeneration policy, EC funding has been used to resource the personal development model of the learning society. In many of the projects we visited, it was difficult to differentiate between the training and personal development aspects of the work. Guidance was fully integrated into a client-centred education and developmental approach. While the third sector providers in Germany were largely untrained in guidance but took an holistic approach to the development of the client, in the Scottish case study, the providers were fully trained professional guidance staff. Guidance was prioritised in this area of high unemployment and industrial restructuring as a mechanism for assisting the long-term development of the area and its people.

This contrasts with one of other case study countries, Italy, where guidance services are used far more by localities to assist in the development of community projects. This corresponds to the social capital model of the learning society, where the guidance worker is regarded as a partner in social development rather than the expert.

In all our case study areas we saw a mix of the models applying, but usually there was a dominant model informing the type of provision informed by the nature of funding available; this in turn was shaped by broad strategic goals. The models of a learning society in operation are clearly cultural constructs informed by economic circumstances and the stability of the labour market, and the nature and extent of disadvantage and how it is understood. Throughout, the EC plays a role through offering the lure of resources to underpin guidance activities where the nature and form are left undefined. Hence while the EC may be operating, according to its White Papers, with one dominant model, individual Member States and public, private and third sector providers within them are able to access and expend these resources in accordance with their own models of a learning society.

Notes

[1] This paper draws upon an Economic and Social Research Council (ESRC) funded project *Adult guidance and the learning society*, which is part of the *Learning Society* programme (Grant No RC1105). We are most grateful to Cathy Bereznicki, Chief Executive of the Institute of Careers Guidance, A.G. Watts, Director of the National Institute for Careers Education and Counselling, and Frans Meijer of the University of Leiden, for their input to the project.

References

Banks, J.A.G., Raban A.J. and Watts A.G. (1990) 'The single European market and its implications for educational and vocational guidance services', *International Journal for the Advancement of Counselling*, vol 1, pp 275-94.

Collin, A. and Watts A.G. (1996) 'The death and transfiguration of career – and of career guidance', *British Journal of Guidance and Counselling*, vol 24, no 3, pp 385-98.

Commission on Public Policy and British Business (1997) *Promoting prosperity: A business agenda for Britain*, London: Vintage.

Commission on Social Justice/IPPR (Institute of Public Policy Research) (1994) *Social justice: Strategies for national renewal*, London: IPPR/Vintage.

EC (European Commission) (1994a) *Growth competitiveness employment: The challenges and ways forward into the 21st century*, Luxembourg: Office for Official Publications of the European Communities.

EC (1994b) *European social policy: A way forward for the Union*, Luxembourg: Office for Official Publications of the European Communities.

EC (1995) *The European dimension in vocational guidance*, Luxembourg: Office for Official Publications of the European Communities.

EC (1996) *Teaching and learning: Towards the Learning Society*, Luxembourg: Office for Official Publications of the European Communities.

Field, J. (1997) 'The European Union and The Learning Society: contested sovereignty in an age of globalisation', in F. Coffield (ed) *A national strategy for lifelong learning*, Newcastle: Department of Education, University of Newcastle.

Fukuyama, F. (1995) *Trust: The social virtues and the creation of prosperity*, New York: Free Press.

Hutton, W. (1995) *The state we're in*, London: Jonathan Cape.

Keep, E. and Mayhew, K. (1996) 'Towards a learning society – definition and measurement', *Policy Studies*, vol 17, no 3, pp 25-232.

Le Grand, J. and Bartlett, W. (eds) (1993) *Quasi-markets and social policy*, London: Macmillan.

Levitas, R. (1996) 'The concept of social exclusion and the new Durkheimian hegemony', *Critical Social Policy*, vol 16, no 1, pp 5-20.

Meijers, F. (1997) 'Adult guidance services in the Netherlands', Paper presented to the ESRC 'Guidance services and the learning society project' seminar, held at University of Bristol, September 1997.

Petan, R. (1994) 'The development of IT in guidance – a response from the higher education sector', in NCAET/CRAC/NICEC (eds) *The future use of Information Technology in guidance*, Coventry: National Council for Educational Technology.

Putnam, R.D. (1993a) *Making democracy work: Civic traditions in modern Italy*, Princeton: Princeton University Press.

Putnam, R.D. (1993b) 'The prosperous community: social capital and economic growth', *The American Prospect* (Spring), pp 35-42.

Rainbird, H. (1993) 'Vocational education and training', in M. Gold (ed) *The social dimension: Employment policy in the European Community*, London: Macmillan.

Rees, T. (1998) 'Social exclusion and equal opportunities', *International Planning Studies*, vol 15, no 1, pp 15-34.

Rees, T., Bartlett, W. and Watts, A.G. (1999: forthcoming) 'The marketisation of guidance services in the UK, France and Germany', *Journal of Education and Work*.

Reich, R. (1992) *The work of nations*, New York: Vintage.

Storey, D. (1994) *Understanding the small business sector*, London: Routledge.

Watts, A.G. (1995) 'Applying market principles to the delivery of careers guidance services: a critical review', *British Journal of Guidance and Counselling*, vol 23, no 1, pp 69-81.

Watts, A.G., Guichard, J., Plant, P. and Rodriguez, M.L. (1993) *Educational and vocational guidance in the European Community*, Luxembourg: Office for Official Publications of the European Communities.

Wilson, P.A. (1997) 'Building social capital: a learning agenda for the twenty-first century', *Urban Studies*, vol 34, no 5-6, pp 745-60.

3

The comparative dimension in continuous vocational training: a preliminary framework

Isabelle Darmon, Carlos Frade and Kari Hadjivassiliou

Introduction

Continuous vocational training (CVT) as an identified and formalised field of policy and practice is a recent creation, and by no means a settled one. Informal training in the workplace, as well as codified training through apprenticeship, has, of course, existed for centuries in most European countries, where it was associated with forms of control of access to the crafts and to mechanisms of social promotion at work (Winterton, 1994). However, even though structures of social dialogue and funding were initiated by the State and established both in France in 1959 and in Britain in 1964, CVT has taken on a radically different aspect in the last 30 years, and mostly in the last 15 years, during which it has become associated with a different kind of change, that is, *change and restructuring for competitiveness and flexibility*. Although the rationales of social promotion, and even that of permanent education as a right still survive, clearly the rationale just mentioned has become dominant and has meant a change in the main players as well, as the *enterprise* became the key decision maker in relation to the implementation and use made of CVT. This change has slowly evolved throughout Europe (Kaiserbruger et al, 1996).

Thus CVT has become a sphere of its own over the last decades, with its legislative and bargaining frameworks, its markets and providers, its quality standards, and has become an issue of considerable expenditure. Directly linked to the search for competitiveness and the problem of unemployment, CVT has become an issue in European and national policy, as well as an object of formal or informal bargaining between policy makers, social partners, and within companies themselves. In short, *CVT is everything but a neutral and mechanistic response of companies to objective market pressures and technological changes*. It has become a key sphere of negotiations (in the broad sense of the term) at different levels, which themselves reveal emerging or renewed forms of regulation, or at least 'social checks'.

To compare CVT innovations in Britain, France and Spain, which is one of the purposes of the Tavistock study on *Innovations in CVT in the workplace*, of which this paper is a contribution, is to analyse evolving modes of *regulation and compromise (or accommodation)* within three societies which have all been subjected to de-regulation, although arguably to very varying extents. This paper sets out the preliminary steps towards what could become a framework for transnational comparisons of CVT, and draws on previous comparative research done by the Tavistock (see especially, Frade and Darmon, 1996 and 1997; Darmon et al, 1996). In the section on levels of analysis in the comparative framework, the main rationales for a framework emphasising the policy background of CVT and CVT as a sphere of negotiation are explained, and the implications for a transnational comparison are drawn out. In the third section we review the main trends of the national configurations of CVT in each of the countries in this study. Finally, we outline the implications of the framework for the transnational comparison of training innovations at the level of the firm.

In the rest of this paper we will refer to 'company training' when discussing the *object* of analysis; we will refer to CVT or 'continuing training' when discussing *policies*. CVT is broader than just company training in most countries – in Britain, where there is no official definition, CVT seems to encompass training for the unemployed in official texts; in France CVT – as defined by the 1971 law and subsequent amendments – includes company training, the right to training leave, and special fixed-term contracts for young people including the provision of vocational training in firms and in schools; in Spain, CVT – as defined by the National Tripartite Agreement – includes company training, the 'individual remunerated training permit' and theoretical training in the apprenticeship contract.

Levels of analysis in the comparative framework

The last three decades have seen dramatic changes in international competition, in the capital ownership of production, in modes of production, and as a result, in employment structures and conditions, forms of work organisation, and skills. The industrial, social, and educational patrimonies of old Europe, which had started to be established in the second half of the 19th century and had been consolidated in the after war period, have been deeply shaken by this international turmoil. Change and flexibility have become masterwords in our societies. In that context, company training has been seen *both* as an instrument for and as a buffer against change, an *ambiguous status* which denies the concept any neutrality.

With these international trends concerning all European countries (and indeed all Western countries), and with the elaboration of European level responses in terms of regulation and de-regulation of competition, quality norms, and consumer protection, one may doubt whether company training, increasingly considered as an instrument for business strategy, may not be more influenced by these trends at the international and European level rather than shaped by the national context. The setting up of international quality standards in some sectors has led, for example, to new training requirements for the workforce of these sectors which have given rise in some interesting cases to training modules being elaborated jointly by the profession in various

European countries, or to the transfer of sectoral training from one country to another (see, for example, Tavistock Institute et al, 1996). However, these very examples have also exposed the complexity of joint efforts and of transfer processes because of national specificities.

In fact, because of the scale of the changes which have occurred in the last three decades, and of the challenges which they have brought to the industrial base and to the welfare systems in our societies, governments have tended to harness efforts for competitiveness and to engage in reforms of the welfare state which have meant high levels of intervention and dramatic changes in the legislative and regulatory frameworks. And these reforms have profoundly affected the role assigned to education and training. Hence it is argued that a transnational comparison of what shapes company training has to start with a *comparison of national policies* – and we would add, not only with education and training policies, but with the wider economic and social policy and the associated regulatory framework. Sectoral de-regulation policies, as well as the de-regulation of industrial relations and of the labour market all have a crucial bearing on company training.

This acknowledgement of the primary relevance of the national policy level in comparative research has been vindicated by the regulation school (eg, see Leborgne and Lipietz, 1990). Although we share some of their key assumptions, we would tend to analyse the general trends in Western societies as more than just a crisis in Fordist modes of production, and refer more generally to globalisation, massive unemployment and the crisis of the welfare states as the major interrelated trends which Western societies have to face. Secondly, instead of having an almost exclusive focus on distinct national 'models' of response, we emphasise not only the communality of the policy trends but also the different national responses on the basis of diverse national institutional mixes and traditions. Thus, we argue, all countries have followed a de-regulatory path, but some more intensively and extensively than others; likewise, the importance of 'checks' to this process is very much to do with national traditions. As we shall see, the institutional arrangements, dominant orientations, and forms of company training are strongly determined by de-regulation and counterbalancing policies.

Thus, the second level of analysis is that of the '*CVT sphere*' at a national level as a sphere of new social 'compromise' within the de-regulation context. The various actors, their interests and the *dominant* terms of the debates are described for each national configuration – these various aspects being quite strongly shaped by the extent to which de-regulation policies have been applied and how they have been checked.

Finally, the third level of analysis, that of the firm itself, will provide a particular instance of company policy, which, again, cannot be considered as a mechanistic response to a set of given objective conditions, but as a particular instance of social 'compromise', marked by company-, sector-, 'territory'-specific characteristics, to be sure, but nevertheless feeding into the wider negotiations taking place in our societies.

Thus the approach developed in this paper seeks to avoid the trap into which in our view too many comparative exercises fall. Too often such comparative exercises are mere mechanical juxtapositions, and seem to be, perhaps unwillingly, underpinned by an axiom that elements or components of innovations have meaning and function in themselves, that is, independently of the *configuration* within which such components are actually included. To this atomistic view we wish to oppose a *systemic view* according to which *the relationships between innovation components and the system within which such components function is far more important than the components taken by themselves.* As will be developed below, for example, the 'compromise' taking place around company training in the UK is *wholly encompassed by economic values* – the dominant one being the free-play of the markets. In contrast, while company training in France and mostly in Spain will be analysed as a 'social compromise' between increasingly dominant market values and still legitimate and powerful social forces, acting as guarantors of employee protection, promotion, and rights, as well as of more general solidarity embracing the unemployed.

De-regulation policies, social checks, and CVT in Britain, France and Spain: a preliminary analysis

In this section we explore the national configurations at a preliminary stage, against the backdrop of common trends towards *economic de-regulation, de-regulation of the labour markets* as well as *decentralisation and de-regulation of industrial relations*; we are primarily relying on a review of the literature, and on previous research carried out by the Tavistock Institute (especially Frade and Darmon, 1996), on preliminary interviews for the fieldwork in this project, as well as on recent fieldwork carried out for related projects. This analysis, however, will be adjusted after completion of the case study work in Britain, France and Spain, specifically planned for this study.

United Kingdom

In comparing dominant policy trends, we would tend to locate the UK at one end of the spectrum, whereas Spain would be at the opposite end. The peculiarity of UK policies, most authors agree, is that the economic aim has become an overarching and dominant concern. Policy priorities have been set up in the UK according to this dominant economic concern, and welfare-social protection in particular has been subordinated to it, to the extent that "even where attempts are made to incorporate social regeneration more centrally into programmes the change of emphasis shifts because *it is integrated into a business oriented vision*" (Cochrane, 1994, p 123; emphasis added).

De-regulation of the labour market in the UK has practically touched upon all those processes which are considered to hinder the free working of the supply side factors in relation to the labour and production process, including any form of association, and particularly trade union power; wage regulations and pay bargaining arrangements, the objective being to individualise pay bargaining – here institutions that influenced pay in the public sector have been removed; likewise, wage councils agreements which covered some 2.5 million workers were also abolished (Mullard, 1995).

UK Regulatory framework

According to different studies the regulatory framework in the UK has been based upon a major institutional strategy and a chief institutional instrument, namely, the promotion of an *enterprise culture* and the creation of what have been called *quasi-markets*. The latter are constituted by quasi-markets internal to a socioeconomic sector – for example, the 'provider market' in the National Health Service, the internal market in education (in continuing training, the main relevant institutions are Training and Enterprise Councils [TECs] and Local Enterprise Companies [LECs] in Scotland). The regulatory framework is also characterised by the *complete decentralisation of industrial relations* (no obligation for employers to recognise unions, no obligation to bargain, no obligation to set up elected bodies representative of staff), although some of the Conservative reforms in that area are likely to be reversed by the new Labour government.

Regulatory framework for company training

The company training sphere is itself characterised by its extreme decentralisation, as a result of de-regulation policies in this area as well. In 1964, in a totally different context of skill shortages, the Conservative government set up a statutory framework in the Industrial Training Act to establish tri-partite Industry Training Boards (ITBs) in various sectors. The following administration (Labour) implemented the new framework and the related levy on all employers. However, pressures (mostly from small and medium-sized enterprises [SMEs]) in the 1970s and the new Conservative agenda from 1979 led to a complete overhaul of the system: "Since ... 1979, the emphasis has moved from tri-partism and statutory training provision towards employer-led and voluntary arrangements for training" (Winterton and Winterton, 1994). The Employment and Training Act of 1981 abolished 17 out of the 24 ITBs and established 90 (now 120) non-statutory Industry Training Organisations (ITOs) in their place, which were employer-led bodies with no obligation to involve trade unions.

However, the pervasion of the training sphere by the enterprise culture has been more far-reaching than the de-regulation of institutional arrangements, and

has also shaped the aims and the contents of company training, in a move which concerned the whole of education and training. As is well known, this evolution started before the 1979 Conservative government with the famous 'Great Debate' in education initiated by the then Labour Prime Minister, James Callaghan. From that time onwards, education was to be "publicly redefined as a mere instrument of the economy" (Frade, 1996). In terms of content, this came to be achieved through 'radical vocationalism' and the assessment of competences defined by educationalists and employers (unions were also invited to take part in most cases).

The overall concern with training for flexibility and adaptation to business circumstances, although ironically delivered through a system usually described as extremely bureaucratic, is best understood when reading official statements such as the definitions provided by the UK in a European Commission publication on CVT (Ant et al, 1996):

*Initial vocational training aims to provide young people with training leading to National Vocational Qualifications (NVQs) and with the broad-based skills necessary to become **flexible and self reliant employees**. CVT follows this initial vocational training phase and is designed to respond to the needs of the individuals and employers **in adapting to changing responsibilities, employment patterns, work roles, technological change and innovation**. (authors' emphasis)*

Although other rationales for company training exist, we will argue in the next section that they share key assumptions regarding the nature of the labour market and of company flexibility. In contrast to practice in Spain and France, British companies do not make a compulsory contribution to the training of the unemployed. This is left to companies' 'corporate social responsibility' strategies, and hence to the discretion of scattered initiatives.

Spain

At the opposite end of the spectrum is Spain, where the *social* aim of the policies of the last two decades has been as important as the *economic* aim. The special situation of Spain is due to the coming of a democratic regime and, with it, the need to develop the emerging, status-influenced rather than universally-oriented, welfare state created during the previous 40-year-long political period. Thus, whereas France and the UK already enjoyed a universal welfare state by the mid-1970s, Spain had to develop and *universalise* it – a task which was to be an essential aspect of the legitimisation of the new democracy. As a result of this, monetarist and de-regulatory policies in Spain went hand in hand with welfare–social protection policies which have established universal services in the areas of health, education and the protection of elderly people.

As compared with the UK, de-regulation of the labour market started timidly in Spain in the early 1980s, with legislation allowing the hiring of workers on temporary contracts (1984). Partly, this timid beginning can be attributed to the fact that labour costs in Spain throughout the 1980s were lower than in other industrialised countries (Almeda and Sarasa, 1996), but also to the power and legitimacy of the unions, which were fundamental in bringing democracy. De-regulatory policies began to be pursued in a more determined way in the 1990s, particularly with the reform of the labour market in 1994. Legislation since 1990 has considerably weakened employment protection, particularly with the creation of different modalities of temporary and apprenticeship contracts. The 1994 Act also allows those companies which are in a difficult economic situation to leave branch agreements. Further de-regulation, together with other compensatory measures, have been undertaken as part of the national agreement between employers and unions at the beginning of 1997.

Spain's regulatory framework

The construction of a democratic political regime and the development of democratic institutions have constituted the main change in Spain over the last two decades. Devolution of power to the autonomous nationalities and regions has undoubtedly been the most important political process, so that a genuine process of political and socioeconomic decentralisation took place, changing profoundly the structure of the previous centralist and authoritarian state. Another crucial process, as mentioned above, has been the re-construction and development of the welfare state. Overall, the Spanish regulatory framework can be characterised by the decentralisation of powers to the regions and

to the localities as well (note that this is utterly contrary to the process undergone by Britain over the last decade); conflicts about overlapping competencies by central, regional and local governments; lack of appropriate coordination structures to deal with such problems; a civil society whose strongest institutions are the family, foundations and charities, particularly the Church, and a voluntary sector which is increasingly more important.

The 1994 reforms of the socialist government cannot be understood if de-coupled from a parallel review of industrial relations, and indeed as we shall see below, social dialogue structures are a key ingredient of the Spanish regulatory framework.

Industrial relations are quite recent in Spain since free unions only re-emerged after Franco's death. The major concern then became the consolidation of democracy, and governments until 1984 helped with the development of structures involving the social partners. After 1984 and the first reforms of the labour market, the 'moderation pacts' which had prevailed until then gave way to a less consensual social compromise which evolved into outright conflict between 1988 and 1992 as the socialist government led a so-called 'rigour' policy. At the same time centralised bargaining was supplemented by sectoral and territorial bargaining. The 1994 Act on the reform of the labour market confirmed this trend by transferring key areas of labour legislation (including Franco's professional ordinances – ie, sectoral labour regulations) to branch and company negotiation. Collaboration over training could be significant as an important step in the evolution of industrial relations and thus constitutes – here again – a sphere of high stakes.

Regulatory framework for company training[1]

Collective bargaining also gained strength within continuing training: in December 1992 a national tripartite agreement was signed which some key principles and practices (see Durán López et al, 1994). Among the most important of these, the agreement established that

- the tax for vocational training, levied on both employers and employees, should, as a mandatory duty arising from the 'principle of solidarity', devote 50% of the funds thus collected to the *Instituto Nacional de Empleo* (INEM) for the training of the unemployed, while the remaining 50% will be devoted to continuing training;

- continuing training should be considered both as an economic factor and as a means of promoting the professional and social development of the employees;

- continuing training is a responsibility of both employers and employees, whereas the role of the government is to support and facilitate the process, and to collaborate on more specific aspects such as the use of the networks of public centres of vocational training.

The importance of the solidarity principle as an essential foundation of the Spanish regulatory framework is thus made manifest. The FORCEM, the institution in charge of allocating the mutualised funds upon presentation of individual or collective company and sectoral training plans, is jointly managed by employers and unions and governed on the basis of consensus. Sectoral and regional commissions were also set up.

France

In France there have been, over the last two decades, 'two voices', as it were, arguing for competitiveness and social solidarity respectively. Since the late 1970s, and apart from the 1981-82 period, policies have been strongly directed at modernising and restoring the competitiveness of the French economy through the enterprise and market principles, and this policy has been accompanied by a social discourse. It has been argued by some economists, however, that employment policies were, to a large extent, subordinated to these economic goals. Nevertheless, the concern about the rise of job insecurity, poverty and exclusion amidst fears of a social divide, brought about policies for monitoring and limiting deregulation, and for extending and increasing social protection to populations 'missed' by sectoral policies and social security institutions. Combating exclusion has become a major national concern, a major topic in government discourse, and has led to the definition and implementation of solidarity principles and mechanisms.

'Flexibility' became the key-word for companies, employer representatives and, of course, for government since the early 1980s. Although this tendency has by no means been as actively promoted by French governments as in the UK, it has in practice been supported by it (Gautié, 1993, p 87). Thus the Labour Law (*droit du travail*) has grown over the past years to include more and more derogatory measures: new labour contracts have been offered particularly to young and long-term unemployed people, and in general more flexible labour contracts have been permitted (Join-Lambert, 1994). While these de-regulatory measures were progressively taking place, although not without hesitations and U-turns, regulations were issued aiming at avoiding abuse and making firms more socially responsible (obligation of *plans sociaux*, parity of conditions for part-time staff etc).

France's regulatory framework

According to different studies, the last 15 years have been marked, apart from a short-lived nationalisation policy, by a *relative* weakening of the state in the economic sphere. This has been translated into a *decentralisation* of the state, which has been arguably more important over the last few years. In particular, the regions have acquired powers to formulate and implement policy in the field of vocational training. It has been argued that the way of doing things in France, that is, the policy-making process, is "statist in style, corporatist in form and pluralistic in practice" (Freeman, quoted in Hantrais, 1990, p 52), a description which seems to capture the spirit of the French regulatory framework. In terms of employment policies, the government has retained responsibility until recently (*loi quinquennale* of 1993, in which some of its prerogatives were decentralised at a regional level), and is still prominent in the education field. The structures for *implementing* policy are, at least in theory, largely decentralised to *collectivités territoriales* and to both sides of the industry, although the state takes the lead when negotiation at this last level is not conclusive.

Framework for company training[2]

The framework for continuous training is in many ways a reflection of these more general evolutions. Donzelot (1984) recalls how all the laws on 'social guarantees' since the beginning of the 1970s, including the one on continuous training in 1971, stemmed from the realisation after 1968 of the necessity of less centralised and 'ideological' fora, and of more local decentralised procedures to tackle the desire of the French to '*changer la vie*' in a concrete and everyday fashion (in this the successive governments have been following Delors' inspiration). The 1971 law thus established the company (and to a lesser extent the branch) as the place of negotiation, decision making and implementation of continuous training. On the other hand, the already mentioned concern with both promoting modernisation *and* addressing social cohesion was already present in the 1971 law, and was re-emphasised in the new 1991 provisions. This is apparent in the various arrangements of the law both in terms of funding (1.5% of the company payroll has to be spent on training their staff and the young unemployed – or paid to a mutualising fund) and of the objectives outlined by the Code of Labour: 'ensure economic efficiency' ... 'combat social exclusion and promote social advancement' ... 'foster cultural development'.

The evolution of the framework for continuing training also reflects the evolution of the role of the state: the initiative was taken by the social partners who agreed on an 'interprofessional agreement' in 1970, which was then translated into law and the same procedure occurred again in 1990/91 – the social partners have a general responsibility for initiating policy in the field. Moreover, the evolution of state intervention in the economy more as a catalyst than as a prescribing authority has been very much felt in the area of company training, for example, with the setting up of '*Contrats d'Etudes Previsionelles*' (studies funded by the government and agreed with the sectoral social partners helping to identify the likely evolution of employment and skill requirements in a given sector and leading to training policy in that sector).

The terms of the debate and the nature of the social 'compromise' over company training

In order to understand what shapes company training in a comparative way, we have argued that we should look at company training as *a sphere which both reflects and promotes new 'compromises'*. Our review of national configurations has shown that the common trends towards economic and labour market deregulation, as well as the decentralisation of regulatory frameworks, had exerted contrary pressures on company training, but that these pressures nevertheless meant that training had become a key area of formal and informal negotiation. Company training studied at the level of the firm is bound to be underpinned by these conflicting rationales and the case study work about to take place in the three countries will have to assess exactly in what terms the question of company training is posed at the level of the firm, both to illustrate and to adjust our more global understanding. In the three countries considered it looks as if flexibility, be it labour market or internal functional flexibility, has become an imperative for which only compensations can be negotiated – company training having become a key element in this compensation strategy set out by unions and/or public authorities. We have also argued, however, that company training was both used/claimed as an instrument for change and as a buffer against change – and the analysis at enterprise level should provide instances of both.

In the UK, as has been said above, the concern for competitiveness is shared by government, employers and unions and has come to *steer* not only the approach to company training but also to initial education and training.

In broad terms, the drive for competence-based vocational training promoted by the government, as well as the exhortations of the Confederation of British Industry (CBI) are met by the dramatic change of attitude of the Trades Union Congress (TUC) (and affiliated unions) over the last decade. There are indeed disagreements, the unions advocating qualification-oriented training, the recognition of qualification in pay, and ultimately the establishment of a right to training and of a levy on employers. Employer bodies, and above all individual companies, might be much less concerned with the actual qualifications, and more with the immediate relevance of training to their business needs.

Despite these disagreements, we would argue that the approach has become consensual at the policy level. Training is an important component of an emerging discourse dominated by 'one voice', wholly encompassed by economic values, on the need for '*flexibility and employability*', flexibility being understood both as 'external' (ie, having to do with hiring and firing, outsourcing, subcontracting etc) and 'internal' (ie, flexibility of working times, internal mobility of workers, multi-skilling etc). The complete de-regulation of the labour market is a fact acknowledged by all actors in the field including the unions, and the re-establishment of a minimum wage and of union recognition requirements will not fundamentally change this fact. "*There is no going back*", union representatives told us in recent fieldwork. Thus this new discourse on flexibility and employability legitimises the already well-advanced shift of the burden of responsibility for education, training and employment on to the *individual*, and implicitly denies any notion of objective structural problems such as lack of jobs, and the increasing proportion of poorly paid, untrained, routine and insecure jobs. It also legitimises the domination of labour market relevance as *the* criterion of the 'good', to the detriment of any educative or developmental goal.

It must be said that this *pensée unique* has been reached within a context where unions have been considerably weakened, where they have had to fight for their survival as meaningful social actors and have had (and still do) to re-think their strategies. More and more unions are entering so-called 'partnership approaches' with employers; there are union 'mergers'; a chief concern is to raise membership. In very general terms, and with notable differences from one sector to another, unions have tried to squeeze into a scene largely dominated by employer concerns, and to found a new legitimacy based on economic 'realism' and managerial competence.

The nature of the consensus also needs to be looked at in a closer fashion, as it may not address the large disparities which exist between sectors and segments of the workforce:

- Economic de-regulation and de-regulation of the labour markets have not hit all sectors in the same ways. Some sectors particularly in industry still enjoy relatively stable and 'rich' industrial relations, steady investment, good levels of pay and social benefits, and have remained relatively impervious to *external* flexibility (ie, to outsourcing, resorting to short-term and temporary contracts etc). In such contexts, such as the chemical industry, for example, the trade off seems perfectly plausible: "The unions have agreed to multi-skilling where workers are trained to the appropriate national standards and competences, which are seen as protecting workers from skill dilution" (Winterton and Winterton, 1994, pp 20-3).

At the other side of the spectrum, the service sectors in particular have been fully experimenting with the joint effects of economic and labour market de-regulation; the pressure for cost cutting and profitability has been such that even in sectors such as banking, where the industrial and social patrimony had been relatively conservative and peaceful until the late 1980s, a complete change of culture and work organisation took place (a process not yet completed) accompanied by massive redundancies, increased centralisation of decision and Taylorisation of part of the work, and polarisation of the workforce (core/periphery, highly skilled/ de-skilled, etc). In these circumstances, and with the looming prospect of a strong decline in the numbers employed over the next 10 years (current estimates are of a decrease of more than 25%) the flexibility/employability balance does not appear so much a trade off as a trap.

- The discourse on flexibility and employability does not take enough account of the current processes of polarisation of the workforce into on the one hand, a high-skilled core, able to bear and take advantage of labour market flexibility; and on the other hand, a less skilled or unskilled periphery, on which labour market flexibility is imposed, and for which training 'for employability' is pure rhetoric.

- Finally, even within this rationale of employability and flexibility, there is a need for serious reflection on the most suitable institutional arrangements. Not only does the current voluntaristic and business-led system take a short-term view of business requirements while the development of broad-based education rather than narrow vocational training might be more suitable for these very interests (for a critical discussion of this issue, see Forrester et al, 1995).

In *France*, as could be expected, the same disparities between sectors, company sizes and sections of the workforce are to be found. However, our concern here is with the *dominant* terms of the social 'compromise', and the case studies will help identify the extents and variations in its application. In a first approximation, one might say that the dominant trend is towards a *trade-off between flexibility and security of employment*. Hence, despite current trends towards training for employability, the efforts of the government, of the social partners, and of the education and training institutions involved in company training have been towards improving the relationship between training and *employment*. This 'compromise', which takes place in a configuration where economic competitiveness is primary but where solidarity and employee protection are legitimate and effective checks, acknowledges the deficits of a system which up until the mid-1980s was in many ways a 'repair system' in that companies hit by economic de-regulation and restructuring were calling for the help of the state and in particular for funding for the retraining of employees once it was 'too late'. This led to a new focus for government policy in the mid-1980s and an impulse towards anticipation of employment and qualification requirements in each sector as well as within companies, a focus of government policy on SMEs and the less qualified workforce, and a renewed impulse towards employer/union cooperation.

The critical mass and system of compulsory funding of company training, the bi-partite structures set up to monitor employment and training (*Commissions Paritaires pour l'Emploi, Fonds d'Assurance Formation*), and finally the substantial impulse given by the anticipation studies funded by the government have led to company training becoming a key forum of discussion and planning, in which overall consensus prevails – in that field – between government, employers, and unions, under the pressure of public opinion. (This is of course not the case in other areas of negotiation.) *Internal* flexibility is thus promoted, as well as qualifying training especially for the lower skilled and for the young unemployed.

However, while there has been substantial progress in a number of sectors, and although innovative agreements have been signed at branch level, similar disparities to the ones encountered in the UK continue to exist: the sectors most concerned by the flexibility of the labour market (such as retail chain stores, hotel and catering, etc) have traditionally had a seasonal, low-skilled, low-paid workforce, and apart from one or two large companies improving their image and addressing turnover problems through company training, the general picture is at odds with the type of social 'compromise' described above.

Similarly SMEs, although some of them have benefited from the sectoral structuring of the organisation of company training (the *Fonds d'Asssurance Formation* providing advice for identification of training needs, for the design of a *cahier des charges*, for the choice of a training provider etc), are still largely out of the described social 'compromise' – as anticipation is difficult for them, and training often impossible to organise (especially as the French law favours off-the-job training).

In Spain as we have hinted above, company training is part of a wholesale restructuring of the regulations and conditions of employment. In particular, the National Tripartite Agreement on continuing training was signed only months before the 1994 labour market reform, and the relationships between employers and unions on continuous training are thus both providing a test for the increased role of social partners in employment matters, and are probably affected by the parallel negotiation on pay scales and work conditions in each sector as a result of the abolition of the professional ordinances. Inevitably as more sectoral labour agreements are being prepared, the issue of linking company training with qualifications and pay is likely to be raised. (This will be one of the issues to explore further in the fieldwork.)

The use of company training as an instrument for change has been a particularly visible strategy in Spain in recent years. The available literature still depicts Spain as a 'modernising' country, and the recent setting up of a review and a complete overhaul of the vocational training system is read as a national strategy for qualifications on a par with the rest of Europe (see, for example, Ant et al, 1996;

Brandsma et al, 1996; Kaiserbruger, 1997). Company training is seen first as a means for Spain to acquire a skilled labour force and as a means for companies to meet their immediate needs (two aims which can be contradictory). This is especially visible through the comprehensiveness of the system put in place: the compulsory contribution, the mutualisation principle, the award of funding of company training only after reviewing company training plans, and above all the institutional arrangements facilitating the participation of very small enterprises through collective training plans on a local or sectoral basis. All of these are innovative arrangements piloted and monitored on a bi-partite basis, which demonstrate the basic consensus of the social partners on a national strategy of modernisation and qualifications.

The unions are keen, as in Britain and France, but perhaps with more emphasis in Spain, to translate these acquired qualifications into job promotions. One of the problems is the fact that bargaining over classifications is proving a very lengthy process; the translation of this aspiration for recognition of qualifications into career paths is by no means an established procedure. The other rising issue on the training agenda is training for employment preservation and anticipation. Partly because of the recent nature of the framework for in-company training, and partly because the strategy of the unions which have a key role to play in the elaboration of this 'compromise' is still unclear to us, it is difficult to summarise the nature of the 'social compromise' being elaborated around training; this will have to be further explored in the fieldwork.

Conclusion

This paper set out to show that studying innovation in company training on a cross-national basis means comparing emerging 'compromises' within increasingly flexible and de-regulated environments. Company training is at the core of change, since it is used as an instrument for cultural change in companies, as a new form of internal communication, and as a support for the adaptation of the workforce to company needs. It is also considered a buffer against change, through the qualification of individuals, through the anticipation of employment trends and skill requirements. The

fact that company training can fulfil both these roles emphasises its suitability for supporting 'compromise'. However, the nature and workability of these 'compromises' very much depend on the relative strength of the institutional actors. 'Industrial patrimonies' in given sectors and companies might be more conducive than others to accommodation. But policy, whether interventionist or not, is still policy, and plays a key role both indirectly through providing checks more or less on deregulation and directly through initiating an institutional framework of negotiation.

It is clear, for example, that the British 'compromise' is underpinned by shared assumptions regarding the flexibility of the labour market and is therefore totally encompassed by economic values, a configuration which is at odds with the French and Spanish contexts. The French 'social compromise' reflects a concern for checking flexibility, as well as for organising solidarity (eg, with the levy paying for the training of unemployed young people). The more recent framework for company training in Spain seems to have been built from the recognition of the special difficulties there are in drawing very small enterprises and some categories of the workforce within the social 'compromise'. This recognition has led to an attempt at designing the framework on the principles of equity and universality of the social 'compromise' offered by company training, whatever it may be.

Notes

[1] CVT in Spain has to be seen in the context of the 1984 *Economic and Social Agreement* (ESA) between the government, the unions, and the employers, which is the Spanish framework for joint action and social dialogue. In particular, the ESA institutionalised vocational training by creating a *General Council for Vocational Training* (established in 1986 as an advisory tri-partite body) and a *National Programme for Vocational Training* (Royal Decree of May 1993). One of the key principles that the ESA established was that of a single vocational training system, comprising (1) the 'Regulated Vocational Training sub-system' (Formacion Professional Reglada) run by the Ministry of Education and corresponding to initial vocational training; (2) the 'Vocational training sub-system for the unemployed' (Formacion Professional Occupacional), run by the

National Institute for Employment (INEM); and (3) the 'CVT for employees sub-system' (Formacion Professional Continuada) managed and administered by the bi-partite Foundation for Continuing Training (FORCEM).

[2] The major landmarks for the development of the legal and institutional CVT framework in France, as presented particularly clearly in Ant et al (1996), are the following: the 1971 Law established the basic arrangements for CVT which are still in force. (1)Right of all employees to training leave; (2) financial obligation of employers; (3) role of staff representatives; (4) creation of Training Insurance Funds (FAFs). The 1990 Law introduced the principle of the right to qualifications and training credit in order to allow low-skilled people to obtain a basic level of recognised qualifications. The national interprofessional agreement of July 1991 set up, among other things, an obligation to negotiate over CVT at branch level; the law of December 1991 extended the financial obligation of companies to companies of less than 10 employees (0.15% of the pay roll), and increased the level of the financial obligation of other companies to 1.5% of the pay roll. The law of December 1993 introduced the concept of 'training time capital' for the employee, and a 1995 law established funding arrangements for this training time capital (this CVT innovation, which emerged in a particular sector and was then broadened to all of them, is one of the focuses of the case studies of the research).

References

Almeda, E. and Sarasa, S. (1996) 'Spain: growth to diversity', in George and P. Taylor-Gooby (eds) *European welfare policy*, London: Macmillan.

Ant, M., Kintzele, J., van Haecht, A. and Walther, R. (eds) (1996) *Access, quality and volume of continuing vocational training in Europe*, Berlin: Luchterhand.

Brandsma, J., Kessler, F. and Munch, J. (eds) (1996) *Continuing vocational training: Europe, Japan and the United States*, Utrecht: LEMMA BV.

Cochrane, A. (1994) 'Restructuring the local welfare state', in R. Burrows and Loader (eds) *Towards a post-Fordist welfare state?*, London: Routledge.

Darmon, I. and Frade, C., Boukhabous, Z. and Danau, D. (1996) Leonardo project 'PRISM', first report, London: Tavistock Institute.

Donzelot, J. (1984) 'L'invention du social', Essai sur le déclin des passions politiques, Paris: Fayard.

Durán López, F., Alcaide Castro, M., González Rendón, M. and Flórez Saborido, I. (1994) *La Formación Profesional Continua en España*, Madrid: Ministerio de Trabajo y Seguridad Social.

Forrester, K., Payne, J. and Ward, K. (1995) 'Lifelong education and the workplace: a critical analysis', *International Journal of Lifelong Education*, vol 14, no 4 (July-August 1995), pp 292-30.

Frade, C. (1996) *Education and training policies in the UK*, the DELILAH Project, TSER Programme, Brussels: DGXII, EC.

Frade, C. and Darmon, I. (1996) *For the development of a comparative framework in research on social exclusion*, Working Paper, London: Tavistock Institute.

Frade, C. and Darmon, I. (1997) 'Social exclusion: towards a framework for understanding and policy', *Annual Review 1996-7*, London: Tavistock Institute, pp 51-7.

Gautié, J. (1993) *Les politiques de l'emploi*, Vuibert, Points Forts Economie.

George and Taylor-Gooby, P. (eds) (1996) *European welfare policy*, London: Macmillan.

Hantrais, L. (1996) 'France: squaring the welfare triangle', in George and P. Taylor-Gooby (eds) *European welfare policy*, London: Macmillan.

Join-Lambert, M.-T. (1994) *Politiques Sociales*, Presses de la Fondation Nationale des Sciences Politiques et Dalloz.

Kaiserbruger, D., Pincot, B. and Tessier, M. (1996) *Le développement de la formation continue dans les PME; analyse comparative des dispositifs allemands et français*, Délégation à la Formation Professionelle, Paris: Ministère du Travail et des Affaires Sociales.

Kaiserbruger, D. (1997) *Négocier la flexibilité, Pratiques en Europe*, Les Editions d'organisation.

Leborgne, D. and Lipietz, A. (1990) 'How to avoid a two tier Europe', *Labour and Society*, vol 15, no 2.

Luttringer, J.-M. and Rojot, J. (1994) *La formation négociée*, Centre inffo.

Mullard, M. (1995) 'Economic policy options', in M. Mullard (ed) *Policy making in Britain*, London: Routledge.

Tavistock Institute, Danish Technological Institute, Bernard Brunhes Consultants (1996) *Final evaluation of the FORCE programme*, vol 1, London: Tavistock Institute.

Winterton, J. and R. (1994) *Collective bargaining and consultation over continuing vocational training*, Moorfoot, Sheffield: Employment Department.

4

Inclusion and exclusion: credits and *unités capitalisables* compared

Pat Davies

Introduction

This paper arises from the project 'The impact of credit-based systems of learning on learning cultures'. The project is not primarily a comparative one; rather it has a comparative dimension designed to introduce a different cultural perspective on policy and practice and thus develop a better understanding of the impact in the wider social context. The paper begins by briefly locating the two credit systems historically and goes on to examine differences and similarities in purposes and practices. It explores the impact each is having on education and training for adults, particularly excluded groups, and finally it identifies some of the current policy debates which are likely to shape future developments.

The main focus of the research in England is the National Open College Network (NOCN) system of credit-based learning, in particular, the London regional Network – the London Open College Network (LOCN) – and definitions and explanations will reflect this. Similarly, references to France will reflect the systems in use in the Nord/Pas de Calais region, particularly the *Université des Sciences et Technologies de Lille I* (USTL). These are case studies which are being used to draw out more general and generalisable issues and trends.

Origins

England

The NOCN credit system began in the North West of England in the late 1970s, was established in London in the early 1980s, and was formalised into a national Network in 1991 (Davies, 1996). The regional Networks do not deliver education and training; their role is that of an accreditation agency offering external quality assurance and enhancement services to providers, and the award of credit backed up by information and records of achievement to learners. Each Network is a local consortium including universities, Further Education Colleges, adult education, voluntary sector organisations, trade unions, TECs and private sector employers.

The roots of most Networks lay in adult and Further Education (FE): they were designed to promote new forms of curriculum, both in terms of content and assessment, for adults who were traditionally under-represented in education and training and who had few or no formal qualifications (UDACE, 1989). Frequently provision was intended to empower learners, particularly women, and to do so through valuing – giving credit to – forms of learning which had not previously been formally recognised, for example, the learning which takes place in a parents' and toddlers' group (Harford and Redhead, 1989). To some extent the Networks intuitively located the credit-based learning within a radical educational practice concerned to empower disadvantaged groups to become more active and effective citizens (Webb, 1991). Thus, in Coffield's terms (1997), the system was firmly located in the democratic imperative.

However, in the 1980s the economic imperative became dominant in all policy areas, epitomised by the development of NVQs and the new funding arrangements for FE which privileged vocational and excluded non-vocational provision. While the Networks had always had a vocational dimension (Lucas, 1986; Mager, 1989; Browning, 1989) and had pioneered much of the work on learning outcomes and alternative forms of assessment, the funding changes further shifted the focus of practice away from input (content) and towards output (learning outcomes). In parallel, the policy position of the national organisation focused increasingly on the need for a credit framework in which all achievement and qualifications could be located. In general, therefore, the NOCN system of credit originated in the democratic imperative – empowering excluded groups for effective citizenship – and has increasingly taken on board the central policy push from the economic imperative, including excluded groups in the labour market. Despite its claims to radicalism, its focus on disadvantaged groups puts this approach in what Silver (1994) called the 'specialisation paradigm', since it is rooted in a notion of social exclusion resulting from discrimination, market failures and unenforced rights (Cousins, 1998).

France

The curriculum structures in the Nord/Pas de Calais region have their roots in wider reforms of the early 1970s, following the riots of 1968, and were greatly influenced by the work of Schwartz (1969; 1973) on initial vocational training for young people, and the committee headed by Lesne (1969) in relation to the education and training of adults. Schwartz (1981) was concerned not only with vocational training per se but with the wider issue of the social exclusion of young people and the need to find new ways to promote their inclusion in the labour market – *l'insertion sociale et professionelle*. A system of *unités capitalisables* (*UCs*) was perceived as a contribution to the solution of these problems. It was proposed in the vocational and continuing system (*formation continue*), rather than in the academic system (*formation initiale*)[1], partly because the latter was, and remains, much more difficult to change, and partly because the need for reform was based on the inability of the mainstream academic system to adequately prepare young people for work or adults to cope with technological, economic and social change. However, Schwartz (1969) was also concerned to develop the skills of learning to learn

and of autonomy in learning to enable individuals to be effective members of society.

The establishment of such a system in USTL and its partner institutions in 1968 was led by the then president who created institutional structures (Louchet, 1971) able to develop a range of programmes for *formation continue* at sub-degree level preparing students for higher education and/or for use in the labour market, for example, the DAEU[2], as well as offering the first cycle diploma and other university qualifications all in modular (*unités capitalisables*) format.

In general, these polices were rooted in the economic imperative but were also seen as having the potential for much wider social change rooted in the democratic imperative. The strategy for dealing with social exclusion is a clear illustration of what Silver (1994) called the "solidarity paradigm", based on integration into a framework of national diplomas which confer social and economic rights in the Republican tradition.

Models and characteristics

Robertson (1994) defined three kinds of credit system: 'impositional', where a numerical partition is superimposed onto an existing course; 'compositional', which begins with units of learning time which can be accumulated into a qualification; and 'competence', which uses learning outcomes and statements of competence as the building blocks of a qualification (epitomised in NVQs). The significance of these different models, for the comparison here, lies in the degree of flexibility and status they derive from their origin and structure – a feature to be dealt with later in this paper.

The English Open College system of credits began as 'compositional' with a standard tariff based on student learning activity expressed in notional time – 30 hours of learning. While retaining this numerical base and the flexibility of accumulation and transfer, it has recently moved towards the 'competence' model based on learning outcomes and assessment criteria and away from a model rooted in programmes of study. It thus now has characteristics of both and might therefore be called a 'combinational' model.

The French system of *unités capitalisables* is much closer to Robertson's 'impositional' model: a pre-existing curriculum, usually in the form of a national diploma, defined in terms of knowledge content or objectives, which has been divided into sections – similar to the idea of a module in the English context. The modular programme tends to be an adapted version of the traditional programme with each module measured in terms of contact hours thus linked to input (albeit expressed in terms of objectives as well as content) rather than to output. Recently, students have increasingly been enroling for a single or small number of *UCs* rather than the whole diploma, and therefore the system is beginning to take on the characteristics of the 'compositional' model.

These models are underpinned and reinforced by a number of characteristics which are important to their flexibility and status which is discussed briefly below and summarised in Annexe 1.

Assessment and level

The role of assessment in the English model is crucial since the assessment criteria, along with the outcomes, are at the heart of the definition of the learning rather than an adjunct to it. Thus the techniques are able to be, indeed must be, very diverse to reflect a wide variation in modes of achievement; and they are based on a pass/fail only: the learner has either achieved the learning outcomes or not. In the French model, the range of assessment techniques is narrower. Although compared to the traditional form of a diploma, which relies entirely on examinations, there is much more continuous assessment (*contrôle continue*), it tends to take the form of small classroom-based tests rather than more individualised techniques and is unlikely to include observation unless laboratory work is involved; and the grading system is the same as the traditional diploma.

Both systems include the idea of level, but very differently defined. The English OCN system is based on 4 levels, each of which has a descriptor designed to reflect the degree of complexity, of learner autonomy and the required range of achievement. Importantly, however, it contains no reference to any particular qualification or curriculum content and can therefore be applied to

any form of learning. The French system, on the other hand, defines the level of a module in terms of its sequence in the curriculum, connected to the idea of a year of full-time study. It depends significantly on the *Baccalauréat* as a marker between lower and higher levels, but is overlaid by a system relating to work and the labour market. So in academic *diplômes*, levels are defined in terms of years either before or after the 'Bac'. In vocational training and continuing education the levels are defined in terms of the posts which require that level of qualification and the posts are defined in terms of the qualification, a system reinforced by the relatively strong link between training, qualifications, position and salary level. It is familiar to students, teachers and employers alike, and has instant recognition and a general applicability.

Both in terms of the assessment arrangements and the level descriptors therefore, the English system is essentially an 'output model' – tightly coupled to assessment and to externally defined notions of level – while the French is an 'input model' – tightly coupled to curriculum and to internally defined notions of level. The former has, potentially at least, greater flexibility than the latter.

Accumulation

The NOCN system of credit provides two modes of accumulation. The record of achievement (often called the credit record) is updated regularly – at least once a year – and may include details of credits achieved in a range of different settings over a long period of time (in principle, a vehicle for recording lifelong learning). Although there have been attempts to adopt a standardised format, it remains essentially a private portfolio until it is accepted by others for some purpose. The second mode is a 'qualification' based on agreed packages of credits approved by relevant members of the consortium and recognised nationally[3]. Importantly a 'qualification' includes a credit record, but the credit record does not necessarily include a 'qualification'.

In the French model, students receive a formal notification that they have passed the *unité(s)* with a particular grade/mark but there is no record of achievement of the NOCN kind. Nevertheless, to have evidence of study and of achievement of some modules 'at the level' is important since it has considerable significance in the job market and in access to FE and training. However, the main mechanism for accumulation is the *diplôme* which, by definition, is 'national' or 'nationally recognised'; the modules derive their public status from these pre-determined qualifications approved by the state and in the case of vocational diplomas, also by employers and the *branches professionnelles*.

In both systems accumulation is publicly and privately managed: publicly within a framework of qualifications, more diverse and decentralised in England and more centralised in France; and privately through the assembling of evidence, more formalised in England and more informal in France.

A system of transfer

In England, the transfer of credits (or indeed any other kind of qualification) depends on the exercise of institutional rights: the institution accepting the learner for further study, has the right to accept or reject the credits achieved by the student previously or elsewhere. Hence there is a need to establish arrangements for mutual recognition and the development of various kinds of consortia – such as the NOCN – to manage and monitor such arrangements. However, this only provides a mechanism for facilitating recognition; it provides no guarantees that any institution will accept the credits, neither does it provide a mechanism for recognition of other kinds of credit or other kinds of qualifications. Hence the OCNs have been at the forefront of the development of a credit framework (Wilson, 1993; 1994) to enable the accumulation and transfer of parts of different qualifications into individualised packages with more widespread recognition in the public domain.

In the French system, the *UCs* (or indeed any other parts of or even whole *diplômes*) have no transferability beyond that which is defined by statute. Since *diplômes* are national, the specification includes the entry requirements and the elements which go to make up the qualification. Similarly jobs and salaries, especially in the public sector, require particular kinds of qualifications set out in national agreements. Although this has become 'looser' in recent years, it remains tight by comparison with the flexible labour market of the UK. Statutes also define a whole range of

equivalences administered by the providing institutions as guardians of the national diplomas; but individual rights are also underpinned by legislation (1985 and 1992) which sets out the arrangements for the accreditation of prior and work-based learning – *validation des acquis* (*VAP*) (Davies, 1997a; Davies et al, forthcoming; Feutrie, 1997).

While *VAP* is not the same as a credit framework, it performs a comparable, and arguably a more comprehensive, function since it allows for not only the transfer of learning, wherever it takes place, but also the transformation of that learning into part of a qualification with nationally recognised status. This can be used to engage in further education and training or can be taken back into the workplace and used to access improved employment conditions and employment rights. The significant distinction between credit transfer and *VAP*, however, is that the former is based on institutional rights and is voluntary, while the latter is based on individual rights and is obligatory.

Credits and *UCs* in practice

Participation

A prime purpose of both credits and *UCs* is widening participation in formally recognised learning, among groups who have traditionally been under-represented. In principle this should be relatively easy to evaluate quantitatively since all institutions in France and the UK are required to collect data in forms which can be aggregated at national level. In practice in the UK, the matter is far from straightforward (Davies, 1997b), especially when the focus of interest cuts across sectors – adult, further and higher education – or age groups. In France, data for academic and vocational qualifications and for *formation initiale* and *formation continue* are collected on a different basis, and despite statutory obligations on institutions to return statistics on the extent of *VAP*, these are not available; a special survey was necessary to establish the extent of implementation in universities (DGES, 1996).

Thus, in both the research case studies – USTL and LOCN – the assembling, aggregation and secondary analysis of data have been similarly problematic.

What is reported here represents extracts from the data assembled and should be read as indicative of each system, similar in some respects, but not directly comparable[4].

Table 1: Learner registrations with LOCN in 1995-96

Sex	%	Age	%
Women	65.1	19-25	26
		26+	64
		Younger or not known	10
			100

Employment status	%	Ethnicity	%
Unemployed	18.8	Bangladeshi	5.5
Unwaged	41.1	Black African	15.6
Employed	16.3	Black Caribbean	8.1
Not stated	23.8	Chinese	1.8
	100.0	Indian	2.4
		Pakistani	1.5
		White	36.8
		Other	12.0
		Not specified	12.0
		Not known	4.3
			100.0

Source: LOCN database (N= 19713)

Table 2: Learners registered for UCs within the DAEU[2] at USTL in 1994-95

Sex	%	Age	%
Women	62	Up to 25	19.8
		26-35	52.6
		36+	27.6
			100.0

Employment status	%	Nationality	%
Unemployed	26.1	French	95.0
Employed	56.4	EU	1.0
Retraining scheme	12.1	Other	4.0
'Unwaged'	5.3		100.0
	100.0		

Source: CUEEP database, USTL (N= 2267)

While some of the data definitions are different, it is clear that both systems are attracting a high proportion of women, unemployed, adult learners. In the UK context, there is clearly a high proportion of ethnic minorities; in the French context such data is not collected (the closest proxy available was nationality), but there is a significant proportion of non-French/EU among the participating students – particularly in the under-25 age group. In general, then, both systems seem to be widening participation.

The comparison, despite its problems, is useful because it highlights the problem of cause and effect. As indicated above, the systems are different in important ways which might be expected to produce different results and yet both seem to be having a similar impact on participation. Clearly, other factors play a part: in particular targeting and funding are important. In the case study colleges in London, when switching to credit-based provision, priority was given to programmes targeted at disadvantaged groups, such as refugees and speakers of English as a second language; and the funding formula functions as an incentive to recruit unemployed people and to record students as being unemployed. In USTL, the student profile is, to a large extent, defined by regulations set out in the statutes; and since the provision is, by definition, *formation continue*, it is not free so that sources of funding are significant. A key source for unemployed people is the *Conseil régional* and for those in employment it is most frequently employers who support the students, through their 'company training plans' which are obligatory. These tend therefore to shape the employment profile of the student body. In both contexts it could be argued that the participation profile is as much the product of targeting and of the financial incentives built into official policy as it is of the structure of the provision. Clearly, in both cases the timing of the course has to be such that the individual can participate (for example, in the evening) but this does not necessarily require a UC or credit-based structure, even though such a structure may make it easier to manage. The social profile of the learners appears therefore to be more the result of effective targeting facilitated and promoted by credit systems, rather than a direct consequence of that structure.

Progression

The question of progression is difficult to map, partly because the data systems are developing behind the practice, and partly because in systems designed to facilitate the accumulation of small steps of learning over a long period of time, it is not possible to follow a large number of learners in a short time-frame. It is clear, however, that the patterns expected and promoted in the two contexts are different. In the French context, while the expectation is that people will increasingly engage in lifelong learning, we have found no discussion about progression which is not linear and always upwards. In the OCN context, on the other hand, there is considerable discussion, linked to the idea of a credit framework, about patterns of progression which do not involve a student in always undertaking credits at a higher level. Nevertheless, the data systems, the funding mechanisms and the national training targets continue to promote a notion of improvement which is based on 'higher' qualifications, so that it is by no means clear that data will be collected or reported about students undertaking 'lower' qualifications.

Flexibility and status

A key purpose of both the credit-based system and the *UC* system is flexibility: in both countries; the lack of it has been identified as a barrier to participation and progression and the response is to construct systems of learning which can be modified to accommodate the needs of individuals and groups who would otherwise be unable or unwilling to engage in formal learning. Flexibility in education and training has nevertheless always been a problematic concept, for example, Ardoino (quoted in Aubégny, 1986, p 123) criticised *UC* models on the basis that they were "*plus souplement fermé au changement*"– more flexibly closed to change – than other arrangements. In the French system in practice, flexibility tends to be limited to timetabling (evening, weekend and block provision) and timing (the ability to vary the pace at which the programme of study is undertaken). While some continuous assessment is possible, there is little choice over the way in which the *UCs* are combined, since this is defined by the national requirements of the *diplôme*, but there is considerable

effort – although this varies between types of course and the situation of the student – to individualise the curriculum through its application to the particular work situation. In some respects, the *UC* version is a more integrated experience than the *classique* version: since the groups are much smaller the tutor has a more holistic view of the individual's learning. In addition, there are reservations about the limits to flexibility in terms of the status of the *diplôme*: for example, in several cases limits had been put on the length of time allowed to accumulate the necessary *UCs* because the very slow pace of some students was perceived as conferring a second–class status on the qualification. Similarly, the recent increase in the number of students who take one or two *UCs* either for specific purposes or as a way of filling gaps identified in the *validation des acquis* procedure, was perceived as difficult to manage since it was often interpreted by others as non-completion and it tended to reduce the total number of *UC* enrolments, thus creating the impression of falling demand and calling into question the continued existence of the programme.

The *UC*-based provision endeavours to deal with the problem of exclusion embedded in French *diplômes* but carries with it an attention to status which threatens the flexibility it seeks to develop. The mechanism of *validation des acquis* is a further attempt to create greater flexibility while maintaining the status of the provision through the codification of the conditions and regulations. In addition, staff are striving to strike a balance between the two in the arrangements which lie within their competence. Rather unexpectedly, the French model of flexibility might therefore be seen as somewhat pragmatic.

In the NOCN context, there are in principle no limits to the flexibility of credit accumulation at the individual level and indeed our research indicates that at the organisational level, providers, particularly employers (although the number involved at the present time is still small) are most keen on this feature: they claim it is this ability to shape the programme to the needs of the organisation and/or the individual that has prompted them to adopt this framework rather than, for example, NVQs. Similarly for individuals, it provides in principle the opportunity to create a package of units and credits and a portfolio/record of achievement to meet their specific needs. However, while confident themselves in the quality and standards of the credits being achieved, some concerns were expressed by staff and students about the status of credits in a situation of competition for places in higher education, for jobs or for promotion. In addition, managerial imperatives tend to limit flexibility in practice and much provision continues to resemble a 'course' rather than an 'individual learning programme'. A further issue arises from the OCN principle that the award of credit in any programme is voluntary – students are not obliged to put themselves forward for assessment and if they do so successfully they are not obliged to claim the credits they have achieved. Coupled with institutional factors, this tends to produce low measures of achievement which are rather difficult to explain. Thus, rather as in the French context, an open, democratic model of flexibility presents problems of justification in the political domain.

The way such issues are worked through by staff is important since they are at the heart of the inclusionary and exclusionary policy and practice. The principle of flexibility in the credit system promotes inclusion but at the same time threatens status, not because different is worse (although there are still traces of that argument even among FE staff), but because unlimited diversity inhibits widespread social understanding of the value of the award and thus limits its currency in the qualifications market and in the labour market. The proposal for a credit framework is designed to deal with this problem: to provide a way of making sense of and valuing any particular unit of learning.

In general then, the USTL system is less flexible but has higher status and the LOCN system has greater flexibility but lower status. It is important to note that in both models, neither the flexibility nor the status is fixed – both are fluid. The model which is therefore emerging is one in which there is always a moving compromise, a balance to be struck in the design and to be maintained in the practice, between flexibility and individualisation on the one hand, and status and currency value on the other.

Given the fluidity of this balance the role of institutions is clearly very important. In England, where such developments are at the discretion of the institutions, this role is obvious. In France it is

less so, but it is clear that, despite legislation creating individual rights, institutional change was slow to take off in relation to *UCs* and continues to be slow in moving to the next stage (Davies et al, forthcoming). There has been little pressure from the demand side, since individuals are unlikely to attempt to exercise their rights if they are unaware of them. In both contexts therefore, committed individuals and institutions are crucial to promote and market the procedures and to change the culture. While a great deal of effort is employed in 'spreading the word', the rapidly changing financial and resource base and the uncertainty which it creates is perceived as a constraint on development in the London context. In France, the debate is rather more political, in the sense that it revolves around ownership of accreditation arrangements rather than institutional resources, although that issue is never far away. Thus, while there is evidence of change, there are few indications of widespread cultural change.

Future directions

The major lines of policy for the future have been suggested already. In the UK the focus of attention is on the development of a credit framework and there are a number of subtexts to the debate which have yet to be resolved. The question of level has been and remains problematic, not only in the literature (Avis, 1991; Parker, 1993; Hyland, 1996), but also in practice as our research shows. There is also the perceived need to widen the curriculum for young people (Dearing, 1996) which is still outstanding. For adults, there is a similar concern about the relationship between academic and vocational, but here the solution is not seen in terms of the integration of vocational and academic but in providing a mechanism for people to access 'small steps in learning' as a means of widening participation, at the same time to accumulate these small steps, to combine them in different ways and to give them legitimacy in the qualifications market and in the labour market. A national credit framework has replaced a national credit-based curriculum as the answer to these problems and has recently been given an additional official push by the Kennedy Committee (Kennedy, 1997), which located it firmly in both the economic and democratic imperatives.

In the French context, there is no policy push towards a credit framework – there is no need for one since the *diplôme* serves that function. However, the development of *VAP* in both the secondary sector and in the universities has raised a number of issues which will be important in the future. First, although this is a weak strand at present, there is a perception that further reform of the curriculum of formal education and training, academic and vocational, is necessary. Second, and this is where the more fundamental change may take place, is the growing consensus that the world of work has already changed and will continue to change (despite a strong resistance to flexible labour markets), and in ways which require a complete rethink of the role of *formation continue* (Delcourt and Méhaut, 1995; Méhaut, 1996; Parlier, 1996; Barbier et al, 1996). From this analysis flows considerable support for the idea of accreditation of work-based learning (De Virville 1996), but as this develops as a policy objective among the various social partners, a struggle is emerging over who should be responsible for such arrangements among the formal education and training institutions, the employers, the trade unions and the *branches professionnelles*. Although social exclusion is understood as a multifaceted concept, at the heart of it in the French context is exclusion from the labour market and therefore notions of inclusion in education and training, present and future, are located in that field.

In both countries the tensions which have been discussed here, between flexibility and status, between diversity and legitimacy, and the attendant political struggles, arise from the attempt to create a qualifications system which is inclusive rather than exclusive and, despite very different approaches from different starting points, exhibits considerable similarity.

Notes

[1] The distinction between *formation initiale* and *continue* is that the former is free and the latter is not, although fees are usually paid by the employer or some form of training grant rather than by the student. It is akin to the distinction between full-time and part-time study in UK universities. However, the label technically attaches to the student rather than to the course.

Annexe 1: A comparison of credits and *unités capitalisables*

	NOCN credit-based system	USTL UC-based system
Origins	Democratic + Economic	Economic + Democratic
Coherence defined by:	Individual within institutional limits	Institution in consultation with stakeholders
Starting point	Learning outcomes	Objectives
Content/input	Less important – a vehicle for delivering outcomes	Important along with objectives
Assessment	Criterion referenced	Norm referenced
	Pass/fail only	Grading
Relative size of 'unit'	Small	Large
Model	Combinational	Impositional
Accumulation mechanism	a) Programme of study leading to a qualification	*Diplôme*
	b) Passport/record of achievement	
Transfer mechanism	Mutual recognition	*Validation des Acquis*
	Voluntary	Statutory
	Based on institutional rights	Based on individual rights

[2] DAEU: *Diplôme d'accès aux études universitaires,* similar to an Access Course in England (Davies, 1995).

[3] The Access to Higher Education Certificate, accredited and validated by the local Network, recognised by the Quality Assurance Agency and approved by the Further Education Funding Council, is an example of such a qualification.

[4] Reforms in the French system and changes in the London database meant that more directly comparable data were not available. The total numbers were different in each database for those variables and years which were most accurate and most comparable.

Acknowledgements

My thanks to Michel Feutrie, USTL, for his help in interpreting both the data and the national policy developments in France.

References

Aubégny, J. (1986) 'Objectifs et management: le système des unités capitalisables', *Education Permanente*, no 85, pp 111-24.

Avis, J. (1991) 'Not so radical after all? Access, credit levels and the learner', *Journal of Access Studies*, vol 6, no 1, pp 40-51.

Barbier, J.M., Berton, F. and Boru, J.J. (1996) *Situations de travail et de formation*, Paris: L'Harmattan.

Browning, D. (1989) 'Open colleges', in A. Rumney (ed) *New directions in vocational education*, London: Routledge.

Coffield, F. (1997) *Can the UK become a learning society?*, the Fourth Annual Education Lecture, London: School of Education, King's College.

Cousins, C. (1998) 'Social exclusion in Europe: paradigms of social disadvantage in Germany, Spain, Sweden and the United Kingdom', *Policy and Politics*, vol 26, no 2, pp 127-46.

Davies, P. (1995) 'France', in P. Davies (ed) *Adults in higher education – International perspectives in access and participation*, London: Jessica Kingsley.

Davies, P (1996) *Choice, rationality and risk in credit based systems of learning: A working paper*, Paper prepared for *Learning Society* seminar, Bristol, September.

Davies, P. (1997a) 'Validation des acquis en Angleterre et en France: une comparaison', *Flash Formation Continue*, no 439, pp 8-10.

Davies, P. (1997b) 'Number crunching: the discourse of statistics', in J. Williams (ed) *Negotiating access to higher education. The discourse of selectivity and equity*, Buckingham: SRHE and Open University Press.

Davies, P., Gallacher, J. and Reeve, F. (1998) 'The accreditation of prior experiential learning: a comparison of current practice in the UK and France', *International Journal of University Adult Education*.

Dearing, Sir Ron (1996) *Review of qualifications for 16-19 year olds*, London: SCAA.

Delcourt, J. and Méhaut, Ph. (1995) *Le rôle de l'entreprise dans la production des qualifications: Effets formateurs de l'organisation du travail*, Luxembourg: CEDEFOP.

De Virville, M. (1996) *Donner un nouvel élan à la formation professionnelle*, Paris: La Documentation Française.

DGES (1996) *Enquête 1995-96 sur la validation des acquis professionnels. Quelle application des textes dans les universités?*, Unpublished paper presented at conference in Lille, December.

Feutrie, M. (1997) *Identification, validation and accreditation of prior and informal learning – France*, Report for CEDEFOP, unpublished.

Harford, L. and Redhead, S. (1989) 'The credentialling of neighbourhood-based adult education – Manchester Open College Federation in practice', *Adult Education*, vol 61, no 4, pp 331-5.

Hyland, T. (1996) 'Access, credit and the learning society', *Journal of Access Studies*, vol 11, no 2, pp 153-64.

Kennedy, H. (1997) *Learning works. Widening participation in Further Education*, Coventry: FEFC.

Lesne, M. (1969) 'Système de crédit et de points. Document', *Education Permanente*, no 3, pp 28-53.

Louchet, P. (1971) 'Le CUEEP de Lille', *Education Permanent*, no 10, pp 51-66.

Lucas, S. (1986) 'Open College: do the ends justify the means?', *Journal of Access Studies*, vol 1, no 2, pp 33-7.

Mager, C. (1989) *Credit where it's due – New routes to success*, Working with Women, Replan National Bulletin no 3.

Méhaut, Ph. (1996) 'Nouveaux modèles productifs, nouvelles formations', *Actualité de la Formation Permanente*, no 142, pp 31-7.

Parker, S. (1993) 'The rise or demise of Access on the post-binary agenda', *Journal of Access Studies*, vol 8, no 2, pp 231-6.

Parlier, M. (1996) 'De l'entreprise qui forme à l'entreprise qui apprend', *Actualité de Formation Permanente*, no 143, pp 8-18.

Robertson, D. (1994) *Choosing to change. Extending access, choice and mobility in higher education*, London: HEQC.

Schwartz, B. (1969) 'Réfléxions prospectives', *Education Permanente*, no 3, pp 1-27.

Schwartz, B. (1973) *L'Education demain*, Paris: Aubier-Montaigne.

Schwartz, B. (1981) *L'insertion professionnelle et sociale des jeunes*, Rapport au Premier Ministre, Paris: La Documentation Française.

Silver, H. (1994) 'Social exclusion and social solidarity: three paradigms', *International Labour Review*, vol 133, no 5/6, pp 531-78.

UDACE (1989) *Open College Networks: Current developments and practice*, Leicester: UDACE.

Webb, S. (1991) 'Access, credit levels and the learner – a rejoinder', *Journal of Access Studies*, vol 6, no 2, pp 205-9.

Wilson, P. (1993) *Beyond 'a basis for credit'*, FEU Consultative Paper, London: FEU.

Wilson, P. (1994) 'Access to higher education and credit accumulation and transfer: option or necessity', *Journal of Access Studies*, vol 9, no 1, pp 10-23.

5

Using 'social capital' to compare performance in continuing education

Tom Schuller and Andrew Burns

Introduction: five senses of comparison

The project on which we report here is comparative in more than one sense. First, the core of the research is the comparison made between performance in initial education and performance in continuing education. We expand on what this means below, but this is obviously not what is generally understood in discussions of comparative research. There are two principal senses which fit more closely to the conventional sense of a comparison between discrete social units located within different national geographical boundaries. The first is between two smaller countries or regions and their larger neighbour within a semi-federal nation. The project compares the performance of both Scotland and Northern Ireland to that of England, in respect of the two aspects referred to above, initial and continuing education. In looking at relative participation and achievement rates, we are taking England as the comparator. This is not because it has particular claims to act as an exemplar of good practice, but because it provides a point or benchmark against which an apparent contrast between performance in initial and continuing education in the other countries can be identified and investigated. However, this comparison with England is at a general level and is used more as a starting point for the detailed exploration of the issues within Scotland and Northern Ireland, including intersectoral comparisons.

The second comparison is a direct comparison between the two smaller countries themselves. The outcomes of the investigations referred to above and described in more detail below, are likely to be different within the two countries (or regions – there is continuing uncertainty over what terminology to use, but there is no doubt about the existence of geographical boundaries delimiting Scotland and Northern Ireland, however contested these may be in political practice). We shall be laying these side by side and examining the differences between them.

A further set of comparisons is at the sectoral level. We have selected five sectors within each of the two regions, and are carrying out fieldwork within each sector, in the shape of focus groups and individual interviews. Again, this is not usually what is meant by comparative research, but it will enable direct comparisons to be made between sectors in the two regions, albeit at a fairly crude level.

Finally, there is a wider and less structured comparative element. We have put together a panel of international correspondents, drawn mainly from smaller countries roughly the size of Scotland or Northern Ireland. This panel is invited to comment on our conceptual framework and on our findings; but also to contribute relevant comparative data from their own country. This is intended to constitute a kind of 'conceptual comparative' dimension plus empirical evidence of a comparable kind; but the comparisons will necessarily only be loosely articulated, depending on the personal commitment of the panel members and the circumstances of their countries, neither of which we were in a position to specify at the outset.

There are, therefore, at least five comparative dimensions to our project, of which at least three and maybe a fourth (but not the first on initial continuing education) conform more or less to the conventional notion of a comparative study. In spite of this, it would be fair to say at the outset that the central focus of the study is not comparative. It is the exploration of the apparent divergence between initial and continuing education in two different societies. Although there is close dialogue between the two research teams and we are influencing each other's approach, the studies are free-standing. To that extent, the research might not qualify as comparative in the fully-fledged sense.

The rest of this paper gives an account of progress to date, viewed primarily from the Scottish side. The next section of the paper outlines the essential background to the current project. The third section presents early insights from the research in Scotland and the final section looks at the issues involved in attempting to measure social capital drawing on international studies. It will be evident that we are not yet in a position to present any comparative results.

Social capital and the *Learning Society*: background to the study

The idea of a learning society assumes that certain types of social arrangements are more likely to promote lifelong learning than others. Yet, although the idea of a learning society has been widely and enthusiastically embraced by politicians and educationalists, there has been little debate over the precise types of social arrangement which promote communication, reflexivity and mutual learning over time (EC, 1995; Ranson, 1994). Specific studies of learning within such social institutions as the family or the workplace have rarely been accompanied by a wider conceptual framework on societal learning.

This project considers the potential of one such framework, that of social capital, to assist analysis of

the social arrangements for learning in two different parts of the United Kingdom. As developed by James Coleman and others, the idea of social capital is beginning to play an important role in helping explain educational attainment (Coleman, 1988; 1994). For Coleman, the concept of social capital complements that of human capital (see also Schuller, 1997); indeed, it helps explain variations in the levels of human capital in any given society. Coleman's conclusion is, briefly, that high levels of human capital tend to arise when individuals can draw on "the set of resources that inhere in family relations and in community social organisation and that ... can constitute an important advantage for children and adolescents in the development of their human capital" (Coleman, 1994, p 300). This is an appealing conclusion, not least because it directs attention to such 'soft' variables as social networks and values, rather than focusing primarily upon the 'hard' variables that tend to form the bedrock of human capital thinking.

This paper gives a preliminary account of how 'social capital' might be used to explain the divergence between performance in initial and continuing education in Scotland and Northern Ireland. The current project builds on evidence from an earlier study undertaken by Naomi Sargant et al (1997) in 1996. The 1996 study was a repetition of a 1990 survey and provides very valuable longitudinal data; in essence it establishes a set of benchmarks for future work on the monitoring of progress towards (or regression from) a learning society.

This is all the more timely as we are possibly on the threshold of a significant change in Scotland's constitutional arrangements. When a Scottish Parliament begins its work in the year 2000, education will certainly figure prominently in the policy issues which it will debate. It is, incidentally, by no means settled how far a Scottish Parliament will seek to intervene in educational affairs, nor how much intervention will be acceptable to local authorities on the one hand, and to the autonomous higher and further institutions on the other. This issue will have major implications for policy and practice in relation to adult participation in education and training. Moreover, the articulation with training policy will also have to be explored more fully.

Comparison with England: background data

The divergence we refer to is between performance in initial and continuing education, in both cases relative to the performance of England. Performance in initial education is measured in terms of qualifications at different levels and of the progression straight from school to further and higher education. In continuing education it is measured primarily using a variety of data on participation in adult learning activities and in training, and on future aspirations to learn.

At the level of myth (Paterson, 1997), and in some respects in empirical fact, Scotland is presented as outperforming England in education. Different national education and training targets have been set in Scotland which reflect higher achievements in initial education. Thus, by the year 2000 the target in England and Wales is for 60% to have achieved two 'A' levels or NVQ level 3 by the age of 21, whereas in Scotland, the equivalent target is for 70%. Less directly relevant to the statistical sources we are dealing with here, but nonetheless significant, is the greater breadth of the Scottish targets, which include references to creativity and citizenship on top of the more entrepreneurial competencies.

The 1996 figures for education and training achievement (see ASCETT, 1997) illustrate this divergence in initial, including vocational, education:

	Scotland	England
a) By age 19 achieved 5 Standard Grades (1-3) or equivalent	78%	69%
b) By age 21 achieved 3 Highers (A-C) or equivalent	54%	46%
c) % of workforce achieving SVQ Level III or equivalent	49%	41%
d) % of workforce achieving SVQ Level IV or equivalent	27%	24%

Turning to adults and looking specifically at the 1996 results from the National Institute of Adult Continuing Education (NIACE), the most significant, for Scotland, is the apparent substantial increase in adults currently or recently participating. Between 1990 and 1996, this rose from 22% to 38%, a rise of no less than 72%. This is the fastest growth

rate of any region, and contrasts dramatically with a UK average rise of just 1%. It brings Scotland from a very lowly position to one that is close to the UK average of 40%. There are no immediate explanations of such a sharp rise, and it is possible that the sample sizes in one or other case – presumably the earlier – were less than adequate. This picture contrasts sharply with Northern Ireland, which has a participation rate of 28%. It is not possible to assess how this rate of participation has increased since 1990, as Northern Ireland was not included in the earlier study. Despite this, the 1996 figure for Northern Ireland is a full 12% below the UK average – a considerable variation in levels of adults participating.

The second observation is less cheering for Scottish eyes. Having apparently caught up to near the UK average, Scotland slides right down the table when it comes to those who are unlikely or very unlikely to learn in the future. A total of 61% put themselves in that category, compared with a UK average of 55%; only Northern Ireland fares worse, with 64%. The overall picture can be best represented by the following figure:

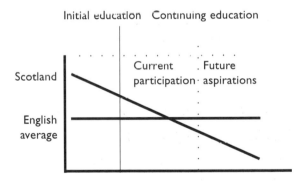

It may be that Scots are simply more honest or direct in their replies, having less fear of appearing to ignore the rhetoric of lifelong learning, but there is no reason to believe that this is the case. More plausible are the arguments that non-formal learning takes place which makes organised learning less of a priority; or, rather differently, that cultural attitudes have a depressive effect on aspirations, at least in some social sectors. We shall be exploring these varying interpretations.

Although Scotland now has an occupational structure very similar to that of Britain as a whole (Scottish Enterprise, 1996), the latest NIACE survey

(Sargant, 1996) shows that Scots fare better when it comes to receiving financial support for education and training from their employers (19% against a UK figure of 13%).

And while the Scots appear from this latest data to be participating in workplace learning to the same extent as their counterparts elsewhere in the UK (15%), the figures from the Labour Force Survey (Winter, 1995/96) suggest that, comparatively speaking, Scotland has a lower propensity to train than might be expected from its labour market structures. These 1995/96 figures are confirmed in the August 1997 Labour Force Survey which shows the UK average for training incidence being 14.4% while the equivalent figure for Scotland is 12.7%.

Initial insights from focus group work

Two main fieldwork instruments are being used: focus groups and individual interviews. The intention, in each country, is to carry out at least one focus group in each of five sectors: agriculture, electronics, tourism, finance and healthcare, and to follow these up with individual interviews. We shall also conduct focus groups and interviews with providers of education and training. We report here on early focus group work in Scotland.

Our experience of the methodology to date has led to a clear position on its utility. We have already found the focus groups to be surprisingly powerful in the range of insights which they generate. In our view they do not provide anything that should be presented as 'conclusions', even in the softest sense (and we are not here using 'soft' in any denigratory sense). They do serve to generate hypotheses and to open up avenues for further exploration, both within the current study – in the interviews and in further desk work – and by others in subsequent research. As such, the use of focus groups has much to offer the policy development process, since it invites dialogue and iteration; it also, as we argue below, can contribute to the theoretical debate by helping the exploration and operationalisation of new concepts.

We are still in the early stages of data collection. Nevertheless, from the focus groups conducted to

date some initial insights are now apparent:

a) *Extended, initial education may not be as productive as it is commonly assumed* in laying the base for a learning society and may not create a strong base for further, continuing education. This has been illustrated through three of the focus groups to date:

- Banking: participants in this focus group specifically stressed that the sector suffers from *education fatigue.* There has been a recent upgrading of the initial qualification levels in financial services. Traditionally the banks recruited 16/17-year-olds, but entry is now largely at graduate level. However, the model is still much the same: graduates come in and begin studying for professional qualifications. Participants voiced a serious concern about fatigue relating to extended examination-led courses, and excessive initial education discouraging people from participating in future.

- Health: participants in this group discussed in some detail the *complacency factor* that they believed has crept into the sector. A large part of this group's discussion centred on Scottish education and how its reputation for high quality may militate *against* levels of uptake in continuing education. Participants discussed how an elite education had given them the feeling that they were superbly educated and therefore did not need any Further Education. Indeed, during this discussion one of the participants made several self-examinatory statements about why he was personally only now becoming aware of the need for, and value of, continuing education. The very success of Scottish initial education, or at least its successful reputation, may limit people's awareness of the need for continuing education. This appeared to be especially true in respect of health/medicine, where the elite factor is obviously pronounced.

- Forestry: participants in this group were quite clear that they believed there was a high level of *dependency* within the sector. The discussion centred around whether individuals in this sector (and throughout wider society) were *citizens* or *clients.* The group believed Scots had inherited an imperialist legacy, followed by a socialist legacy; both of these having left them more as clients than citizens. The participants contrasted this with Denmark and Norway using the example of 'self-build' housing: Denmark and Norway have 20% to 40% of their total housing stock from this self-build category, while the comparative figure for Scotland is a mere 6%. A further example discussed was a large Finnish family firm exporting kits for self-build houses all over Europe; there are no equivalent family (or other types of) production units here in Scotland.

b) The *volume versus quality* argument – again, two of the focus groups undertaken to date have illustrated this point:

- Banking: regulatory requirements have led to *high volume* but a *ceiling not a floor*. Again, it was clear from the participants in this group that regulation is the motor behind the expansion of training within the banking sector, but with ambivalent effects on quality. Financial advisors are now required to meet minimum standards, and there has been an explosion of demand for training to meet these requirements.

  But this turns out to have been a ceiling rather than a floor. The minimum regulatory requirements are met by a three-paper exam, and this is what most people settle for. A consequence of this has been a drop-off in those going for higher level qualifications. In other words, volume growth has been accompanied by a lowering of the level of training, and perhaps also a cultural change, which has less regard for professionalism and more for externally imposed requirements.

- Forestry: the strong presence of health and safety regulations has contributed to *lack of appreciation for 'real' quality skills*. This group discussed in some detail what was considered to be the mass of health and safety legislation which was contributing to a stifling of education in 'real' skills, as members of the group described them. There was a clear culture of 'on-the-job' training, with one participant indicating that this was always preferable to attendance of any course, especially a health and safety course. And unanimously the group members agreed that levels of statutory requirements for health and safety training had led to a consequent lack of training in basic production skills. They believed the skills required to produce a quality product, in an appropriate economic quantity, were no longer being considered as a priority. The

participants obviously considered the high volume of statutory requirements as a 'brake' on the quality of the product they produced.

These brief examples are all drawn from Scottish groups, but most of the points they raise have at least potential application elsewhere, as countries generally declare their intention to extend initial education. All these examples suggest that the relationship between formal educational opportunities and the goal/s of a learning society may be far more complex than first expected – there may even be, as suggested above, an inverse relationship.

An obvious policy conclusion from these initial insights is that we need to pay much more attention to relationships (informal as well as formal) and to what fosters attainment rather than simply providing more opportunities for attainment. All of the groups, to some extent, discussed how we might improve the sharing of information and sharing of values in order to avoid the problems of education fatigue, complacency, dependency, and address the issue of volume versus quality. It is this – the sharing of information and the sharing of values – which we are putting at the centre of our approach to social capital and to which we now turn.

Measuring social capital

We have committed ourselves to exploring the usefulness of social capital as a concept possibly fundamental to a better understanding of the relationships between the different forms of learning which contribute towards a genuine learning society. The concept is proving to be itself problematic for a number of reasons:

- it means quite different things to different people (see, for example, Foley and Edwards, 1997);
- it has a strong tendency to circularity;
- it is hard to measure or operationalise.

Nevertheless, we have found it to be a powerful way of generating a different approach to the conventional human capital approach, especially where human capital is thought of in narrow, individualistic terms and focuses only on qualifications. In this section we provide some illustrative outline of how diverse are the ways in which social capital has been used and some of the measures or indicators used in these different approaches. The examples are drawn from several different countries, raising questions about the cultural specificity of the concept. We then indicate how at present we have chosen to operationalise it.

Robert Putnam defines social capital as "the features of social life – networks, norms and trust – that enable participants to act together more effectively to pursue shared objectives." To demonstrate the decline of social capital in America – the 'bowling alone' phenomenon – he uses membership of many forms of political and social organisation, including political parties, school boards and hobby clubs. He also looks at figures on newspaper reading and TV watching – indeed, these lead him to pinpoint TV as the culprit in the decline of social capital. In some writing, he includes visiting neighbours as a form of social capital, which makes the concept almost impossibly broad.

We should not forget that Putnam developed this approach in a comparative study of regions in the north and south of Italy. Putnam's seminal work does not measure 'social capital' per se. The statistical work is done on a set of indicators measuring '*institutional performance*' – the institution being that of representative (regional) government. The relevant indicators that Putnam uses for this are divided into two broad categories: *policy processes* (cabinet stability; budget promptness; quality of statistical/information services; comprehensiveness, coherence and creativity of policy pronouncements); and *civic community*, where the indicators are as follows: vibrancy of associational life (number of cultural and recreational associations; newspaper readership [following de Tocqueville's stress on the newspaper/civic life link]; electoral turnout; and preference voting, ie, voting for a person not a party [taken by Putnam as an index of the absence of civic-ness]).

Narayan and Pritchett (1996) base their study of social capital in Tanzania on a large-scale survey of 5,000 households. Social capital is defined, following Putnam, as "the density and nature of the network of contacts or connections amongst individuals in a given community." The study starts with a discussion of social capital as a *metaphor*

which fits both parts of the phrase – that is, it is capital, representing an investment with returns, and is social, involving relationships between people. Social capital performance is measured using three dimensions: the extent of membership in groups; the characteristics of those groups of which they were members (kin heterogeneity; income heterogeneity; rating of how well the group functioned); and expressed levels of trust and perceptions of social cohesion. Narayan and Pritchett use the data and the framework to explore the relationship between social capital and income, and conclude that there is a relationship running from higher social capital to higher incomes.

At times, social capital is no more than a fancy name for social networks in a rather crude sense, as illustrated in Meyerson's study of 111 Swedish executives, which looked at how social capital enables a profit to be turned from human capital (1994). The criteria that Meyerson develops to measure social capital are two-fold: managers' work contacts in other organisations; and membership of elite clubs, for example, Rotary, Lions.

With the work of James Coleman we turn to a more specific link between education and social capital. Coleman identifies trust as one fundamental characteristic of social capital, for instance, in Egyptian markets where traders help each other through various forms of mutual obligation, although notionally in competition with each other. Secondly, he points to norms and sanctions which promote or enforce the forgoing of immediate self-interest. Thirdly, there are information channels, and Coleman cites as a prime example the university as an institution fostering social capital – perhaps somewhat romantically depicting a universal sharing of information across departments, faculties and universities. On none of these – trust, norms or information networks – does Coleman provide specific measures.

When it comes to looking at the relationships between formal education and social capital, Coleman defines the latter in terms of the relationship between parents and children – how much effort the former put into the latter's learning, with J.S. Mill and Asian immigrants into the US at the high end, and parents who despatch children off to private school and take no further interest in them at the low end. More specifically, he also uses as indicators the numbers of changes in school due to family residential changes (tearing up the roots of social capital); the frequency of discussions between schools and parents; the presence of both parents and the number of siblings in the house (many siblings and one parent = little social capital). With this framework, Coleman carries out extensive empirical analysis of the relationship between social capital and school achievement, and these or similar indicators have been used in other studies perhaps partly because the requisite data banks were available.

Finally, one example of work deriving directly from Coleman is Teachman et al (1997), using a large sample from the National Education Longitudinal Survey in the United States to examine the effects of various measures of financial, human and social capital on the likelihood of children dropping out of school. They develop a further set of criteria for measuring social capital: attendance at Catholic high school; the number of times a student has changed school; whether the parents know the parents of their child's closest school friend; the intensity of schooling and the related interaction between parents and children. This last is further operationalised using responses to questions about how much parents talk to their children about school, and how many times parents have been in touch with the school. Their conclusions are consistent with Coleman's argument that financial and human capital must be accompanied by social relations which allow resources to be transmitted to and used by children.

Teachman and his colleagues end with a plea for better measures of social capital. We would echo the general conclusion just cited that this does not apply only to parents and children, but also to other kinds of social unit where education or learning are involved. In other words, investment in human capital by an employer or by society requires the appropriate social context in order to be realised effectively (Schuller, 1997).

That very different conceptualisations of social capital exist can be seen from the measures used in different studies claiming to deal with social capital – and we have only discussed a sample of them. In part this makes the concept worryingly diffuse. But

to give it a sharper focus it may be helpful to identify two broad categories:

- *Social capital as an individual attribute:* here, social capital is measured by reference to individual activities and characteristics, for example, membership of clubs, the amount of time spent in various activities, or the consumption of different media forms.
- *Social capital as a function of relationships:* these relationships can be between individuals or institutions. Two rather different examples here are the *poles universitaires* in France, an initiative which pushed universities in the same city to establish closer contact with each other, at least beginning the process of sharing information; and German *Handelskammer*, which give institutionalised reinforcement to local employers' commitment to the value of training.

Such relationships can be measured in a variety of ways. For example, there is a significant literature within organisational studies of network analysis (eg, Wasserman and Faust, 1994) , and in social anthropology on relations of all kinds (eg, Bott, 1971). Again, with such broad application the concept risks spiralling out of control.

We shall be gathering data on individual attributes, mainly from existing sources, and spreading our net reasonably widely. On the issue of relationships, we are continually developing our approach. In the focus groups we put forward a simple pentagram, depicting five agents which could reasonably be thought to be central to the functioning of a learning society: providers of learning opportunities; employers; the state; professional bodies; and individuals themselves. This is of course inadequate to capture the full range – a notable omission is the family – but it does serve to demarcate some of the territory.

We have then asked the groups to focus not on the qualities or performance of the agents but on the quality of the relationships between them. This was not always easy to convey, but in the main worked reasonably well. However, in order to give a sharper focus, we have decided to concentrate on two aspects of the relationship. The first is the *sharing of information:* how far is information shared between the two (or more) parties in the relationship, what are the mechanisms for sharing it, and does it need to be improved. The second is the *sharing of values*: how far do the agents subscribe to the same set of values in respect of learning, how far is this explicit, and what are the consequences.

We have only just begun to apply this approach, but intend to follow it through in the individual interviews as well. So far it is proving very fruitful. We should note that there is no simple assumption that the more information is shared, and the more values are held in common, the better. Relationships can be too close, too cosy, both for the internal functioning of the group or unit concerned (see, for example, Granovetter, 1985), and of course for the wider environment. But the assumption that a greater sharing in both respects would probably be beneficial for promoting the learning society has worked well in eliciting interesting views – as well as prompting further hypotheses and lines of exploration.

Concluding remarks

In the introduction we listed various senses in which this study might be considered 'comparative'. The main comparisons were with England; between Scotland and Northern Ireland; and, more speculatively, with other countries involved through our international panel. In the previous section we discussed our central theoretical concept, social capital, and its application to different societies. Although it is too early to be confident, our estimate is that the different sectors involved will also prove to have, at least to some degree, different cultures which need to be compared if we are to understand the ways in which learning is interpreted and valued across society. This even extends to sub-sectors: forestry as a 'can-do' part of the agriculture sector; IT as the high-speed, no-time corner of electronics; and so on. These characteristisations are clearly simplistic, but they illustrate at how many different levels a comparative approach in the broad sense can be applied.

References

ASCETT (Advisory Scottish Council for Education and Training Targets) (1997) *Advisory Scottish Council for Education and Training Targets Annual Report*, Glasgow: Scottish Enterprise.

Bott, E. (1971) *Family and social networks: Roles, norms and external relationships in ordinary urban families*, 2nd edn, London: Tavistock Publications.

Coleman, J. (1988) 'Social capital in the creation of human capital', *American Journal of Sociology*, vol 94, Supplement, pp 95-120.

Coleman, J. (1994) *Foundations of social theory*, Cambridge, MA: Belknap.

EC (European Commission) (1995) *Teaching and learning: Towards the Learning Society*, Luxembourg: Office for Official Publications.

Field, J. and Schuller, T. (1996) 'Is there less adult learning in Scotland and Northern Ireland? A quantitative analysis', *Scottish Journal of Adult and Continuing Education*, vol 2, no 2, pp 61-70.

Foley, M. and Edwards, R. (1997) 'Social capital and the political economy of our discontent', *American Behavioural Scientist*, vol 40, no 5, pp 669-78.

Granovetter, M.G. (1985) 'Economic action and social structure: the problem of embeddedness', *The American Journal of Sociology*, vol 91, pp 481-510.

Labour Force Survey (Winter 1995-96) *Labour Market Quarterly Report*, November, 1996, Skills and Enterprise Network Publication, London: DfEE.

Meyerson, E.M. (1994) 'Human capital, social capital and compensation: the relative contribution of social contacts to managers' incomes', *Acta Sociologica*, vol 37, pp 388-99.

Narayan, D. and Pritchett, L. (1996) *Cents and sociability: Household income and social capital in rural Tanzania*, Preliminary Version, August, World Bank.

NIACE/GALLUP (1996) *UK Learning Survey*, Leicester: NIACE.

Paterson, L. (1997) 'Traditions of Scottish education', in H. Holmes (ed) *Compendium of Scottish ethnology, vol 11*, Edinburgh: European Ethnological Research Centre.

Putnam, R. (1993) *Making democracy work*, Princeton: Princeton University Press.

Putnan, R. (1995) 'Tuning in, tuning out: the strange disappearance of social capital in America', *Political Science & Politics*, vol 28, no 4, pp 664-83.

Putnam, R. (1996) 'Who killed civic America?', *Prospect*, March, pp 66-72.

Ranson, S. (1994) *Towards a learning society*, London: Cassell.

Sargant, N., Field, J., Francis, H., Schuller, T. and Tuckett, A. (1996) *The learning divide*, Leicester: NIACE.

Schuller, T. (1997) 'Building social capital: steps towards a learning society', *Scottish Affairs*, vol 19, pp 77-91.

Scottish Enterprise (1996) *Scottish Labour Market and skill trends* (Final Report), Glasgow: Scottish Enterprise.

Teachman, J.D., Paasch, K. and Carver, K. (1997) 'Social capital and the generation of human capital', *Social Forces*, vol 75, no 4, pp 43-59.

Wasserman, S. and Faust, K. (1994) *Social network analysis: Methods and applications*, Cambridge: Cambridge University Press.

6

Issues in a 'home international' comparison of policy strategies: the experience of the Unified Learning Project

David Raffe, Cathy Howieson, Ken Spours and Michael Young

Introduction

There is wide support within Britain for a more unified system of post-compulsory education and training, in which the divisions between academic and vocational learning are reduced or abolished. However, the different British systems appear to be pursuing this goal in different and possibly divergent ways. In England and Wales Sir Ron Dearing's (1996) *Review of qualifications for 16-19 year olds* endorsed the tri-partite structure of academic, education-based vocational and work-based vocational pathways, while proposing several measures to link them and to increase the coherence of the system as a whole. His review provides the starting point for the Labour government's consultation about its future policy. In Scotland the government's Higher Still reforms will introduce a unified system of post-16 education in 1999 (Scottish Office, 1994). Thus, in England and Wales academic and vocational learning remain divided into separate tracks, while in Scotland the tracks are being replaced with a unified system. (In Wales, however, the government has recently expressed an interest in the 'WelshBac' proposals, which are closer in many respects to the unified system approach of Scotland – see Jenkins et al, 1997.) All the British systems, however, might be seen as developing or pursuing strategies for 'unifying', or at least linking, academic and vocational learning. None of these strategies have yet been implemented, and in England and Wales the basic strategy for unification is still being determined (Hodgson and Spours, 1997).

These developments in post-compulsory education are the subject of the Unified Learning Project (ULP), a joint project of the Centre for Educational Sociology (CES) at the University of Edinburgh and the Post-16 Education Centre (P16EC) at the University of London Institute of Education. The ULP aims:

- to compare developments in post-compulsory education and training in Scotland with those in England and Wales in relation to the motivations for and resistances to unification and the approaches and strategies being followed;

- to develop the concept of a unified system, to clarify its relationship with the concept of a learning society, and to explore issues in the design of unified systems;

- to develop complementary concepts and understandings of the process of unifying academic and vocational learning;

- to engage with and reinforce the 'learning process' of policy development and implementation.

The ULP is thus centrally concerned with conceptual development, particularly in relation to the basic concept of 'unification' which is neither agreed nor even widely recognised at present. Its initial focus is the macro level of analysis: it wishes to develop concepts at the system and national framework level. It aims to analyse policy strategies and issues in the design and implementation of policy; but since the policies have not yet been implemented the analyses are largely ex ante, in the sense that they cannot be informed by empirical study of policies in practice. Even the policies and the strategies that underlie them have been changing rapidly during the course of the project. All these features of the ULP have raised issues for the design and methodology of the research.

The ULP is complemented by an eight-country European study of strategies to promote parity of esteem between vocational and general learning in post-16 education (Lasonen, 1996; Lasonen and Young, 1998). The Post-16 Strategies project is funded under the European Commission's Leonardo da Vinci programme; it brings together 11 research teams in eight countries, coordinated by the University of Jyväskylä in Finland, with the CES and P16EC 'representing' Scotland and England respectively.

In this paper our main focus is the ULP, but we also refer to the Post-16 Strategies project since the two projects are complementary. In the next section we briefly discuss the purposes of comparison in the project. The central purpose, which underpins the others, is to support conceptual development, and in the following section we describe the main conceptual frameworks which we have developed as the basis for comparison. We conclude by considering the extent to which comparisons have achieved these purposes, and discuss some of the issues that have arisen.

Purposes of comparison

The comparative element within the ULP serves are at least four purposes.

- The first and simplest is to address the main empirical questions of the project: what are the different approaches to unifying academic and vocational learning in the different parts of Britain? How are the different systems developing and are they diverging or converging? These questions can only be answered by comparing the countries of Britain.

- The second purpose of comparison is to support conceptual development. The project aims to develop new concepts to describe variation among systems, to analyse change, and to point to possible models for the future. By placing

different systems side by side we can identify dimensions of variation which we may wish to include in our conceptual framework.

- The third and related purpose is to support policy development, not so much by identifying policies or approaches which can be 'borrowed' by other territories of the UK, but by identifying more general issues and lessons.

- Fourth, and more tentatively, by comparing trends in different countries we may be able to identify cross-national pressures on education systems and analyse the dynamics of social and educational change.

Our comparison is intensive rather than extensive. It covers just three systems: given the interdependence of Welsh and English education, for many purposes it covers just two. Our initial analyses have focused on England and Scotland, and we plan to use Wales as a case study to 'test' some of the conclusions of the two-country comparison. Our approach allows for finely grained comparisons but it does not give many degrees of freedom for system-level analyses.

The comparison is also a 'home international' comparison, among three of the countries of the UK. Elsewhere one of us has argued for the contribution that home international comparisons can make to educational research (Raffe, 1991; Raffe et al, 1999: forthcoming). For example, they may yield more transferable lessons for policy; and they may make theoretical and methodological contributions by challenging the assumptions of the prevailing 'societal' approach. However, home internationals need to be seen as part of a spectrum of comparative research, which also includes comparisons across nation-states with varying degrees of difference. The ULP is complemented by the more extensive approach of the Leonardo Post-16 Strategies project, to the mutual benefit of both projects.

Both the ULP and the Post-16 Strategies project exemplify the collaborative model of comparative research (Hantrais, 1995). Research teams participate as equal partners in the project and each team has prime responsibility for collecting and interpreting data on its own country.

Of the four purposes described above, the second –

to support conceptual development – is fundamental, and underpins the others. It also contributes to another purpose commonly ascribed to comparative research: the better understanding of one's own country. In the next section we describe the conceptual frameworks developed in the project.

Conceptual models for comparing policy strategies

Initial conceptual framework

When we planned the project, in 1994-95, we conceived of the difference between Scottish and English/Welsh developments in the unification of academic and vocational learning in terms of two distinctions. The first distinction was between the 'top-down' reform process in Scotland and the 'bottom-up' initiatives in England and Wales. In Scotland the Higher Still reforms were introduced by central government and their development and implementation were led by national organisations. In England and Wales the Conservative government's resistance to 'A' level reform appeared to have produced a stalemate as far as national policy developments were concerned, but several initiatives at local and institutional level aimed to unify, or link, academic and vocational learning. For example, a number of area- or institution-based projects introduced common components for academic and vocational courses, or devised measures to promote student transfer between the two. There were also some 'unifying' initiatives at national level, such as Credis, the Credit framework for post-compulsory education in Wales.

The second distinction was between the two models of unification which these different developments appeared to represent. In Scotland Higher Still was introducing a unified *system*. In England and Wales the various reforms appeared to prefigure a looser form of unification which we called a unified *framework*. The ULP was planned on the basis of these two distinctions. It would start by reviewing the field, and then proceed to 'map' unifying initiatives at both national and local levels in both countries. Case studies of 10 of these initiatives would examine their concepts of unification and

their strategies for pursuing it, and analyse the issues that they raised.

By the time the ULP started in April 1996, these two distinctions were no longer appropriate; nor was the research design based on them. Many of the local unifying initiatives that had sprung up in the late 1980s and early 1990s had ended, or had reduced their ambitions. Other local initiatives which we had perceived as 'unifying' did not pursue unification as their explicit goal; it was therefore difficult to identify and analyse their strategies for unification. The consensus for unification which some of us had seen emerging in the early 1990s (Young and Watson, 1992) had not resulted in a shared language of unification; without this language it was difficult to engage the help of participants to 'map' strategies for unification. Most important of all, the Dearing review, published in the month before the ULP started, shifted the policy initiative in England and Wales back to the national level. It was now possible to pursue a much more symmetrical comparison of the national developments on either side of the Border.

We re-designed the project to focus on the different 'national policy environments' and policy strategies; instead of case studies of initiatives, the project now includes thematic studies which compare particular issues or themes as they arise within each national policy environment. (These include studies of the merger of regulatory and awarding bodies, of the role of core or key skills, of group awards and overarching certification, and of the work-based route.)

Our main sources of data have been interviews with policy makers and key participants in policy debates and in the development and implementation of policy, observations of selected policy processes (such as the consultation seminars on Higher Still) and documentary sources. Most of the interviews in England have been conducted by the London team, and the Scottish interviews by the Edinburgh team; logistics and time pressures have curtailed our ambitions for joint or cross-border interviewing. We have interviewed people responsible for implementation at local and institutional level, but the effect of the changed policy environment has been to shift our main focus of attention up to the national level. Another effect has been to make the object of our enquiry more elusive: the national policies are still in the process of development so the project has found itself comparing two moving targets.

Current conceptual framework

We have developed a conceptual framework to support our comparisons at national level. This draws on our earlier distinction between unified frameworks and unified systems, but presents these as points along a continuum of strategies and of systems. Post-compulsory education and training systems vary in the extent to which their institutions, curricula, certification, mode of participation, student pathways and other organisational features are based on distinct and separate tracks. This variation can be seen as a continuum, ranging from fully tracked systems to unified systems with no tracks. However, this continuum can also be described in terms of three points along it:

- a tracked system: with separate and distinctive tracks;

- a linked system: with features linking the tracks or common properties which underline their similarity or equivalence (similar to our earlier concept of unified framework, described above);

- a unified system: not a uniform system, but one which accommodates a diversity of provision within a unified set of arrangements, and does not use tracks to organise provision.

A system may not have a unique position on this continuum. Rather, the continuum can be applied to several different dimensions on which systems may vary. Our tentative list of such dimensions is shown in Figure 1. We identify four main groups of dimensions, which respectively describe the content and process of learning, the 'system architecture' of course structure, certification and student pathways, the modes and institutions of delivery, and the government and regulation of the system. For each dimension, Figure 1 describes characteristic features of each type of system. A system need not have a consistent profile across all dimensions. For example, it may have comprehensive upper-secondary schools, and thus be a unified system with respect to the local institutions dimension, but provide distinct curricula for academic and

vocational students and thus remain tracked with respect to the curriculum dimension.

The conceptual framework allows for 'cross-cutting' dimensions which are less easily represented within Figure 1. These include the age range covered by the system (does it cover all adults or does it stop at 19?) and the scope of the system. For example, the unified system to be introduced by Higher Still in Scotland will not include most work-based provision. Arguably it will create a *unified* system of school- and college-based provision but a *linked* system connecting these with work-based provision.

We have used the conceptual framework to map the current English and Scottish systems (Raffe et al, 1998b). In this analysis England represents a tracked system on a majority of the dimensions and Scotland currently represents a linked system. However, there are substantial variations across the dimensions: for example, our analysis places Scotland in the tracked category with respect to assessment and in the unified category with respect to course structure and pathways.

We have also used the framework to analyse policy strategies (Raffe et al, 1998b). Corresponding to the three types of systems, there are three strategies for dealing with the question of differentiation in post-16 education – and, in particular, for addressing problems associated with 'academic drift' and the low attractiveness of vocational education. The first strategy corresponds to a tracked system. It emphasises the separateness of the tracks and the differences between them: if vocational education can maintain or acquire a distinctive ethos, character and tradition, it may avoid being judged by the values of the academic track and escape the low status that this can confer. The second strategy retains different tracks but emphasises their similarities. It promotes the formal equivalence and parity of the different tracks and provides for common structures and elements as well as opportunities to mix or transfer between the tracks. In other words, it aims to develop a linked system. The third strategy would abolish the formal status differences between the different pathways by eliminating tracks and bringing them together within a unified system. Each strategy, therefore, aims to move towards one of the three types of system or to consolidate features of this system that already exist.

Our analysis identifies the post-Dearing policy in England as a weak form of the second (linkages) strategy, and Higher Still in Scotland as a unified system strategy (but with important qualifications, notably the exclusion of work-based provision). But once again our analysis takes account of the dimensions of system change described in Figure 1. Both England and Scotland are moving along the continuum – becoming 'more' unified – in terms of system architecture and in terms of government and regulation. In respect of content and processes Scotland is moving towards unification, but in England the Dearing reforms may even enhance the present tracked nature of the system. In neither system will the structures of delivery change as a planned outcome of the current reform, although

Figure 1: A matrix of unification: types of system and their dimension

	Tracked system	Linked system	Unified system
Content and process			
Purpose and ethos	Distinctive purposes and ethos associated with each track	Purposes and ethos overlap across tracks	Multiple purposes and pluralist ethos
Curriculum	Different content (subjects, areas of study)	Some common elements (eg core skills, general courses) across tracks	Curriculum reflects student needs and integrates academic and vocational learning
Teaching/learning processes	Different learning processes in different tracks	Different learning processes but some common feature	Variation based on student needs and not tied to specific programmes
Assessment	Different assessment methodologies and grading systems	Different methodologies but with level and grade equivalences	Common framework of methodologies including a common grading system
System architecture			
Certification	Different certification for each track	Certification frameworks link tracks, eg overarching diplomas, equivalences	A single system of certification
Course structure and pathways	Different course structures and insulated progression pathways	Course structures allow transfer and combinations	Flexible entry points, credit accumulation, and single progression ladder
Progression to higher education	Progression to higher education not possible from some tracks	Different types of admission from different tracks	All tracks give admission to higher education
Delivery			
Local institutions	Different institutions for different tracks	Variable/overlapping relation of track to institution	One type of institution, or choice of institution not constrained by type of programme
Modes of participation	Tracks based on separate modes (academic/full-time, vocational/part-time)	Tracks partly based on mode	Single system covers different modes
Staff	Different staff for each track, with non-transferable qualifications	Variable/some overlap of staff	Socialisation, qualification and conditions are consistent for all staff
Government and regulation	Different structures for different tracks	Mixed/variable organisational structure	Single administrative and regulatory system

there may be unplanned changes in either direction. Both national strategies can be represented in terms of the direction and distance of planned movement along the various dimensions.

This conceptual framework emerged after a lengthy period of mutual learning, in which we reviewed the current strategies and the debates in relation to the political, social and institutional context of each country. There was also a fruitful interaction between the intensive, two-country comparison of the ULP and the more extensive, eight-country comparisons of the Leonardo Post-16 Strategies Project. The Leonardo project used similar concepts of strategies, which drew in part on the work of the ULP, but it also stimulated the work of the Anglo-Scottish project. It drew attention to issues that tended to be taken for granted in the British research. For example, the wider European comparisons alerted us to the extent that the British reform strategies were qualifications-led, and had come to take the existing institutional structure of post-16 education for granted. It made us aware of the extent to which British debates about linking academic and vocational education have marginalised employer- and work-based provision. An application of the model to Scotland and Sweden led to a further dimension being added, describing pathways to higher education (Raffe et al, 1998a).

The Leonardo project also made us aware of ways in which our conceptual framework might be further developed (Young et al, 1997). For example, the Scotland–Sweden comparison revealed two different emphases within the concept of a unified system. One emphasised individual choice and flexibility, the other emphasised commonality and the achievement by all students of a common level and content of knowledge. These corresponded to the Scottish and Swedish strategies respectively, but we found the same tension in the policy debates within each country, and in the unification debates within England. A second example is the pilot project in the German dual system, represented in the Leonardo project, which drew attention to how our conceptual framework was based on the relationship among tracks and might therefore overlook radical initiatives to integrate general and vocational learning within a track.

Issues in the comparative approach

At the time of writing the project has five months still to run; the data-collection, and many critical stages of analysis and synthesis, are still in progress. In the final section of this paper we offer only a very provisional assessment of the role of comparison in our project. We do so by discussing the four purposes listed earlier.

Comparing approaches and changes in the two systems

The first purpose was to address the empirical questions: what different approaches to unifying academic and vocational learning are being pursued on either side of the Border? How are the systems developing? Here the main methodological problems have arisen from the dynamic nature of the policy process, and from the timing of the project in relation to this process, rather than from its comparative nature. In England and Wales the policy strategy outlined by Dearing is under review. On both sides of the Border policy strategies have been evolutionary: they have proceeded by steps and stages, and have been re-defined as experience of each step is gained. In both systems the main proposals of the current reform programmes have not yet been implemented. Policy development and policy implementation are not discrete stages of the process; policy continues to develop as it is put into practice. At this stage, therefore, any assessment either of comparative policy strategies or of the development of education and training systems is necessarily provisional. However, our conceptual framework gives us a tool with which to analyse the dynamics of policy and system change, and to identify future possibilities.

The fact that the project is analysing policy strategies in the process of development raises several issues for comparative methodology. For example, it makes the project sensitive to the selection of key informants. Policy development is a conflictual and fragmented process: different interviewees have different stories to tell and there is a limit to the triangulation that is possible. The project is also dependent on its access to these informants and its ability to establish the necessary relations of trust. In a collaborative project like the

ULP, each research team acts as a gatekeeper to the key informants and data sources within the system which it represents, and the project is dependent on the team's networks and social location within that system.

A further issue in the analysis of policy development is timing. In Scotland, we have conducted most of our interviews at a point when the main strategic decisions have been taken. The main outlines of the policy are settled and attention has shifted to relatively specific matters of fleshing-out and implementation. In England, we have conducted our interviews during a period when the basic strategy itself is still under discussion. It has not been easy to frame comparable questions in these two policy environments.

Conceptual development

The comparative approach has been most clearly successful in respect of the second, and most important, of the purposes listed above: to support conceptual development. We will not repeat what has been described in the previous section, but would stress that a systematic attempt to analyse the differences and similarities between systems has been a fertile way of generating analytical concepts and frameworks. In particular it has led us to develop the useful idea of dimensionality in relation to unification. Our ability to complement the intensive ULP comparison with the more extensive Leonardo comparison has enriched both projects. Comparisons which only look within Britain may fail to identify the essential features of 'Britishness'; so, too, may comparisons in which Britain or the UK is represented only by England.

In a collaborative project the systematic analysis of differences and similarities referred to above must begin with a process of mutual learning. In the case of the ULP this was organised around the preparation of the project's first Working Paper (Howieson et al, 1997), which compared the 'unification' debates in England and Scotland, and traced the recent history of these debates in each country and related them to their institutional, social and political contexts. Writing this Working Paper occupied much of the first eight months of the project, longer than had been anticipated. Yet it was an essential part of the project's comparative

methodology. European collaborative cross-national projects, such as the Post-16 Strategies project, usually begin with a stage of mutual learning in which the research teams deepen their understanding of each other's systems. (They also usually neglect or underestimate this stage when the project timetable and budget are determined.) However, the mutual learning stage proved equally important in our home international comparison – perhaps even more so, because the similarity of institutional structures and terminology in the UK systems make it easier to overlook the essential differences between them.

Mutual learning is about the research teams as well as about the systems they represent. Each team acts as a gatekeeper to its own system, not only in respect of its networks and social location within that system, but also in terms of the theoretical perspectives, perceptions and values which it brings to the research. In a collaborative project each team is a part of the system it describes. This is more a resource than a 'problem' for comparative research, but it needs to be recognised and acknowledged by the research teams in the partnership.

Policy learning

The third and related purpose of comparison is to support policy development. As far as we can judge the work of the ULP has been favourably received by the policy makers and other users with whom the project engages. There have been positive responses to the consultation seminars organised by the project, to its Working Papers and other written outputs, and to the conceptual frameworks it has developed. However, although users express support for the principle of home international comparisons, in practice their main interest has not been (directly) in the comparative aspect of the project. At each of the first two consultation seminars, held in Edinburgh and London, most discussion focused on the country in which the seminar was located. When we have 'disseminated' more informally – for example, at meetings with policy makers or when fielding questions from our own interviewees – it has again been the specific country rather than the comparison in which users have expressed interest. In Scotland some of our interviewees have encouraged us to use the project to develop a constructive critique of the Higher Still policy process, in the tradition of CES research; in response to this, the two teams have agreed that some outputs of the project should not be directly comparative, but should focus on the policy process or on other issues within each country. Similarly, in England some interviewees have encouraged us to continue to explore issues that take us beyond the inevitable constraints of the current policy process, and which may require a less explicitly comparative approach.

It is easy to understand the reasons for this apparent indifference to the comparative aspect of the research. England and Scotland are at different stages of the policy process, so policy makers and practitioners in the two countries do not share the same immediate concerns. Neither system can yet offer empirical evidence of the effectiveness of the policies concerning unification. In addition there is a reluctance, in both England and Scotland, to accept that anything could possibly be learnt from developments on the other side of the Border.

Comparative research can generate valuable lessons for policy and practice, but these may need to be mediated by the research teams and, more importantly, by the theoretical and conceptual frameworks which they generate from their comparisons.

Analysis of system change

The final and more tentative purpose of comparison is to identify cross-national pressures on education systems and the dynamics of social and educational change. Both England and Scotland are moving to the 'right' in terms of the conceptual framework of Figure 1. England is moving from a tracked to a linked system, and Scotland from a linked to a unified one (although in both cases the extent and even the direction of movement may vary across the different dimensions of change). Across the countries in the Leonardo project, there is a similar tendency to move towards unification; the main exceptions are Austria and Germany which retain track-based strategies. On the basis of these trends we have begun to speculate, on the one hand about the nature of cross-national pressures for educational change, and on the other about the ways in which these pressures interact with the specific institutions, circumstances and politics of each country (Young and Raffe, 1998). Such speculation (and we use this

term deliberately) goes beyond the original goals of the ULP, but illustrates the value of linking the intensive 'home international' comparison of the ULP with the more extensive comparison of the Post 16 Strategies project.

References

Dearing, Sir Ron (1996) *Review of qualifications for 16-19 year olds*, Hayes: SCAA.

Hantrais, L. (1995) 'Comparative research methods', *Social Research Update*, no 13, Department of Sociology: University of Surrey.

Hodgson, A. and Spours, K. (eds) (1997) *Dearing and beyond: 14-19 qualifications, frameworks and systems*, London: Kogan Page.

Howieson, C., Raffe, D., Spours, K. and Young, M. (1997) 'Unifying academic and vocational learning: the state of the debate in England and Scotland', ULP Working Paper 1, *Journal of Education and Work*, vol 10, no 1, pp 5-35.

Jenkins, C., David, J., Osmond, J, and Pierce, J. (1997) *The WelshBac: Educating Wales in the next century*, Cardiff: Institute of Welsh Affairs.

Lasonen, J. (ed) (1996) *Reforming upper secondary education in Europe*, Jyväskylä: Institute for Educational Research, University of Jyväskylä.

Lasonen, J. and Young, M. (eds) (1998) *Strategies for achieving parity of esteem in European Upper Secondary Education*, Jyväskylä: Institute for Educational Research, University of Jyväskylä.

Raffe, D. (1991) 'Scotland v England: the place of "home internationals" in comparative research', in P. Ryan (ed) *International comparisons of vocational education and training for intermediate skills*, London: Falmer, pp 47-67.

Raffe, D., Arnman, G. and Bergdahl, P. (1998a) 'The strategy of a unified system: Scotland and Sweden', in J. Lasonen and M. Young (eds) *Strategies for achieving parity of esteem in European Upper Secondary Education*, Jyväskylä: Institute for Educational Research, University of Jyväskylä.

Raffe, D., Howieson, C., Spours, K. and Young, M. (1998b) 'The unification of post-compulsory education: towards a conceptual framework', *British Journal of Educational Studies*, vol 46, no 2, pp 169-87.

Raffe, D., Brannen, K., Croxford, C. and Martin, C. (1999: forthcoming) 'Comparing England, Scotland, Wales and Northern Ireland: the case for "home internationals" in comparable research', *Comparative Education*.

Scottish Office (1994) *Higher Still: Opportunity for all*, Edinburgh: HMSO.

Young, M. and Watson, J. (eds) (1992) *Beyond the White Paper: The case for a unified system at 16+*, London: University of London Institute of Education, Post-16 Education Centre.

Young, M. and Raffe, D. (1998) 'Strategies for promoting parity of esteem between academic and vocational learning: a comparative analysis', in Lasonen and Young (eds).

Young, M., Howieson, C., Raffe, D. and Spours, K. (1997) 'Unifying academic and vocational learning and the idea of a learning society', *Journal of Education Policy*, vol 12, no 6, pp 527-37.

7

Planning, implementation and practical issues in cross-national comparative research

Antje Cockrill, Peter Scott and John Fitz

The practice of field research is the art of the possible.
(Buchanan et al, 1988)

... the advantages of cross-national research are
considerable, so too are the costs. (Kohn, 1989)

Introduction

Cross-national comparative research in the social
sciences is now becoming increasingly common,
especially within the countries that make up the
European Union. However, specialised study of the
methodological ramifications of such activity is a
rather more recent phenomenon, with contributions
such as the volume by Hantrais and Mangen (1996)
going some way to redress the former neglect. This
paper attempts to contribute further to this debate
by illustrating some of the methodological and
implementation issues for international social science
research encountered during work on a project on
'Training for multi-skilling: a comparison of British
and German experience', funded under the UK
Economic and Social Research Council's *Learning
Society* programme during the period 1995-97.

This investigation has, as the title implies, a strongly
cross-national comparative element. In fact, we
could devise a matrix of potentially cross-cutting
variables, as the project compared training, skills, and
developments towards multi-skilling in three
different economic sectors (the engineering and
construction industries and the residential social care
sector) in one British and two German regions. The
project adopted a 'matched pair' approach, by

marrying up small- and medium-sized organisations
of similar size and product/service in the relevant
regions of both countries which could be visited for
personal interviews based on a semi-structured
interview schedule. By definition, therefore, this
methodology implied a primarily qualitative rather
than quantitative approach, particularly since the
number of organisations (25) it was intended to
study per country per sector is too low to permit
statistically representative results. Nevertheless, such
numbers do still engender considerable problems for
potential matching, as we shall discuss below. The
rest of this paper highlights some principal
difficulties in devising, conducting and analysing the
results of international research work in
organisations, drawing particularly on the
experience of the 'Training for multi-skilling'
investigation.

Devising cross-national studies

The international aspect is, in many ways, both the
most defining and the most difficult of the
comparisons involved in this project. Comparisons
across national borders, particularly concerning
economic or policy issues, are often based on one or
both of the following main motives: to identify best
practice and/or to resolve some current problems in
social theory (O'Reilly, 1996). In this project we
were concerned with 'best practice' in training and
skills provision, but also with policy issues in both
countries.

However, neither of these goals could be achieved
without trying to gain a thorough understanding of

the social and political context in both countries, including the exploration of regional differences. Patton (1987) maintains that qualitative research is naturalistic and holistic, and "assumes that the whole is greater than the sum of its parts". He argues therefore that the understanding of the social and political context of a situation is essential for the overall understanding of that situation.

When dealing with data derived from two nations, this latter point is of considerable importance and presents a major difficulty: to be able to understand fully the social and political context in another country one would need ideally one or more researchers based in the countries involved, not only able to speak the language fluently but who are also immersed in the cultural and political context (cf Lawrence, 1988). Needless to say, this ideal is unattainable for many research projects, although perhaps a valid issue to consider for the future selection and training of researchers as cross-national research becomes more common.

Wiegand (1985) maintains that the difficulties created by cultural and linguistic difficulties and by different settings imply that uncritical adaptations of foreign experiences have to be regarded with care, particularly in a decentralised country like Germany. He concludes as follows:

Doch ist im Grunde in der ernstzunehmenden Forschung immer schon davor gewarnt worden, die Möglichen direkter Übertragung von Erfahrungen aus anderen sozialen und politischen Realitäten allzu hoch anzusetzen. (p 17)

(But essentially there have always been warnings by serious researchers not to overestimate the possibilities of directly transferring experiences originating in other social and political realities.)

In this project we found that this issue of different settings was rather important, for a number of reasons. For one thing, the various regions were at different stages of the economic cycle during the fieldwork period of 1996-97. Whereas certain parts of South Wales, and particularly its manufacturing industry, were undergoing a relative improvement in fortunes, Germany was still suffering the effects of an abrupt down-swing attributable to the declining competitiveness of the German economy, the

impact of the spiralling costs of absorption of East Germany, and the transfer of much production to locations with cheaper unit labour costs. This had affected the more economically successful region of Baden-Wuerttemberg relatively more dramatically than Nordrhein-Westfalen.

Also, both the legal and structural environment in which our interview respondents operated varied considerably not only between the UK and Germany but, in some circumstances, even between regional units. One example of the latter source of variation was training provision in the social care sector, which did not only vary between countries, but also between the two German regions. Furthermore, funding for vocational training within Wales is distributed through the Welsh Office, rather than directly *via* the Department for Education and Employment (as in England and the English regions). This additional layer has allowed the Welsh Office to institute a number of training initiatives at so-called intermediate skill levels (for craft and technical workers) in manufacturing industries that do not exist elsewhere in the UK.

Generally the organisational structures for both initial and further training provision in Britain and in Germany are sufficiently different to create problems of comparability. One apt example is the widely differing roles of the English and Welsh Training and Enterprise Councils (TECs) and the German Chambers of Industry and Commerce (*Industrie- und Handelskammer,* IHK). A large part of the TECs' role is as a conduit for monies for vocational training derived from government. The conception of TECs was itself modelled on the American Private Industry Councils (Bennett et al, 1994) and it is only more recently that some English TECs – influenced inter alia by the German IHK construct – have moved towards merger with local Chambers of Commerce in a bid to expand their local economic development role. What difference lies in a name, however? The German IHK has a very different local position in vocational training to the English and Welsh TEC, whether or not the latter is formally combined with a Chamber of Commerce. The IHK organisations play a central role in the German training system, enjoy a symbiotic relationship with local firms through the system of membership and levies that applies, and are far more powerful than their British counterparts. It is these structural differences which make truly comparative international research difficult: if they are not acknowledged and taken into account, there is a danger that instead of a comparative analysis, a project results in mere juxtaposition. Foskett (1979) outlines this problem:

Juxtaposition is not comparison, and no matter how many descriptions, of even the highest interest, we may record, they still remain descriptions unless we are able to reveal patterns which exhibit similarities and differences, identify their causes and effects, and relate them to other patterns which exhibit similar features in a similar context. (p 4)

It is therefore in this final stage of the project that we have to ensure that our results will be truly compared and not only described as two sets of discrete and unrelated data.

Since this project included interviews in two countries, the interview schedule had to be translated and the interviews had to be conducted in two languages. However, this presented its own difficulties. Rheingold (1988) points out that many concepts are 'untranslatable', that is, they do not have an equivalent in the target language. Furthermore, seemingly similar concepts have different connotations in different languages. Because of these difficulties, a decision has to be taken between literal translation and psychological equivalence. Robinson (1984) makes an important point concerning research instruments in two languages, viz:

*Instruments [for research] should offer **psychological equivalence** to respondents and not apparent objective equivalence to the investigator. To pose the same form of question to two people who are different may require posing that question in two different forms. (p 163)*

In order to achieve psychological equivalence, it is not only necessary to translate the interview schedule but also to adapt it to the different settings. As far as we were able to, we adjusted the composition, questions and phrasing of the schedule to the different environments. One particularly thorny difficulty provides the most outstanding example: the central concept of the whole project, the English term 'multi-skilling', is incapable of

unadapted translation into the German language because of its differing implications within the UK and German socio-industrial *milieux* respectively. No direct equivalent exists as a discrete expression, and there is no simple way of describing its meaning. Eventually, after several unsuccessful attempts, we decided that two German terms came closest to the English concept of multi-skilling, although each is imbued with slightly different connotations. Our lexicon thus included the term *Mehrfachqualifikation*, quasi-literally '*qualification*' (authors' added emphasis) enabling the possessor to do more'; or, secondly, *Hybridfahigkeit*, quasi-literally 'hybrid ability/capability'. Particularly instructive is the idea expressed by the concept of *Mehrfachqualifikation* that additional skill is made transparent through the acquisition of extra transferable qualifications. Such a view can be readily grounded within the German VET system's stress on formal qualification in a state-recognised occupation. Our UK fieldwork confirmed only too resoundingly the lack of importance accorded by employers either to the possession of vocational qualifications by recruits or to the achievement of additional formal qualifications among employees in service.

Conducting international fieldwork

Two possible methods of conducting fieldwork internationally present themselves, each with their own advantages and disadvantages. This choice is similar to the industrial 'make or buy' decision: either one undertakes the whole fieldwork programme oneself, or one sub-contracts some or all of the foreign data collection to an indigenously-based team within each respective country of study (see Rainbird's 1996 discussion). The 'sub-contracting' strategy, of which one of the present authors has past experience (see Bolton et al, 1993; Scott and Kelleher, 1996), allows data collection to be carried out in parallel and overcomes the problem that the foreign researchers concerned may not be sufficiently immersed in the culture and understanding of that nation. It places the principal researchers in the role of remote coordinators and managers, with a more limited engagement with the detailed mechanics of data collection. Regrettably, it brings with it the disadvantages of some loss of control, possible misunderstandings and communication difficulties – not least those engendered in translation – and even clashes between contradictory organisational and political agendas. Another more epistemological drawback is the loss of external insight and fresh perspective on social phenomena which is surely one of the very purposes in undertaking social science research (see Meil, 1992). These problems can be countered if one conducts the foreign fieldwork oneself, as this project elected to do, but leads into a number of other possible obstacles, the most apparent of which are described below.

When we had succeeded in designing satisfactory interview schedules for both countries, we faced the task of planning, organising, and conducting these interviews. We had decided to choose our potential respondents by cold-calling, that is, randomly picking addresses from available trade directories, and matching them in roughly comparable British–German pairs. This approach to matching pairs has a well-known pedigree in industrial sociological research. The National Institute for Economic and Social Research's programme comparing productivity, skills and training in particular industries (see Steedman et al, 1991; Mason and Wagner, 1994; inter alia) and the 'Anglo-German' studies by Warner and his collaborators (see Sorge et al, 1983; Campbell et al, 1989; inter alia) are among the most well-known and respected of such endeavours, although there are now many other examples of the genre.

A reading of such studies (see particularly the methodological discussions in Campbell et al, 1989; Sorge and Warner, 1986; and especially Sorge et al, 1983) suggests the success of this approach in the past when a number of conditions have been met. It works particularly well when applied to very precisely defined industrial segments and when dealing with relatively small numbers of 'pairs' although, even here, Sorge et al (1983) admit to having to endure "a rather lengthy search for matching units". However, our study was innovative in that we proposed to extend it into three broad economic sectors, making the total number of potential sites very large. Furthermore, most if not all of the major studies using this method, including those discussed above, have tended to proceed according to the 'sub-contract'

mode, with an active partner in the respective case study nations charged with conducting fieldwork there. Unusually, our project utilised the 'direct control' approach, electing to plan and organise all project fieldwork from our UK base. This forced us to confront a number of difficulties that would have arguably been less extreme had the alternative method of managing the data collection been employed.

Hence we quickly found that we had to make compromises between precise matching and taking the opportunity for interviews with available firms, even if there were no directly equivalent 'partner firms' in the relevant region(s) of the other country. This is in line with Buchanan et al's (1988) recognition of the necessity for approaches to fieldwork in organisations that are to some extent opportunistic in practice. They maintain that fieldwork is permeated with the conflict between what is theoretically desirable on the one hand and what is practically possible on the other, and conclude that in a conflict between the desirable and the possible, the possible always wins. We found that the difficulties of trying to pursue a 'matched pairs' approach in two nations simultaneously forced us to compromise in order to obtain a sufficient number of respondents in both countries. The data bases we used to match companies across regions of two countries proved unreliable: trade directories and similar lists of addresses contained high proportions of misleading or outdated information, bankrupt or merged enterprises. This aspect was problematic in both countries, but much more so in Germany. Furthermore, cold-calling abroad implied that the legitimisation of our calls was difficult, with international return calls not being an acceptable option. These two factors together caused the loss of a considerable amount of time in simply trying to acquire sufficient numbers of organisations willing to cooperate. We used publicly available directories and lists for all three sectors in Britain, and for engineering and construction in Germany.

The rate of response to initial phone contacts was extremely poor in the construction sector, and therefore we decided not to use this method for care in Germany as well. In this final sector, we approached regional and national organisations with requests for addresses. This method had a longer initial lead time but was far more effective overall than cold-calling. Although not all potential respondents on the organisations' lists participated, the majority did so, and it was a far more efficient way of organising interviews abroad. It can be concluded at this point that cold-calling abroad does work but takes an inordinate amount of time and effort; it is better to establish some contacts first and then ask them for potential respondents.

As for the implementation of the fieldwork abroad, the practical complications of combining research in two countries cannot be underestimated. Apart from such issues as awareness of regional geography and transport links (no incidental matters!), and having to arrange transport and accommodation, fieldwork abroad also usually implies moving around, and thus the inability to counteract cancellations of interviews at short notice became problematic. Even when respondents did try to contact us (several did not and were then unavailable when we arrived), it did not necessarily mean that their message arrived in time. Lengthy fieldwork periods abroad proved expensive for the foreign fieldwork budget at a time of adverse exchange rate conditions, thus we eventually decided to send only one researcher instead of two, as we had done for the first few journeys.

The international angle of this project presented a number of problems and difficulties, many of which were related to the methodologically unusual approach for this type of research of relying primarily on one UK-based team. However, it is also a very rewarding approach to research: to look beyond the boundaries of one national system and its policies and forms of organisation to another national system with a different set of structures and parameters for policy making.

Analysing international data

One of the main difficulties that presents itself to the international researcher looking at skills, training and labour organisation in different countries is the problem of identifying the underlying causes for any differences in the results, and whether effective learning from other countries is possible. We have already pointed out the difficulties in adequately understanding the socioeconomic context of any phenomena explored in different countries.

However, even having attempted to integrate different features of this context in the data analysis, the question remains whether differences between countries are the result of differences in the socioeconomic, or political system or if they are the result of different labour market conditions and labour organisation; or lastly, if they arise from a variety of other factors such as firm size or type of enterprise. Some earlier research has focused on the national contingent differences between systems and societies as the determining factor for companies' structures and organisational practices. Maurice et al's (1986) 'societal effect' model, which has distinct educational, occupational and organisational dimensions, states the case resolutely for the defining role of what Rose (1985) describes as "relatively permanent systemic features specific to named historical societies" (see also Lane, 1989; Maurice et al, 1980; also Steedman, 1988). While we do not intend to go into the relevant theoretical debates extensively here, such issues have been pertinent to two evolving disputes: the first is about convergence – now largely metamorphosed into controversy over globalisation – and the second concerns divergence – now similarly resurfaced in a wide range of studies in different disciplines stressing the continued (and perhaps extended) salience of locality.

Recent international research on industrial organisation (see especially Mueller's 1994a review) is indeed alive with conflict over the respective roles and influences of the firm – particularly the trans-national business (Mueller, 1992; 1994b), of globalising influences, and of the national society. Mueller's studies of working practices in European Ford engine plants lead him to identify trends of convergence between practices in different countries and the importance of organisational factors (albeit in one very large organisation!), while Kelleher and Lee's (1993) four-nation investigations of training in some of the very same plants cause them to temper the discovery of centripetal trends with a reassertion of the very different depth and structures of training encountered. Koehler and Woodard (1997) come to the conclusion that organisational factors are more important at plant and company level but that 'societal effects' seem to be more important in defining the structure of industry and the economy. For the most part, our own research tallies with Koehler and Woodard's conclusion – albeit with some caveats to be discussed further below. To a large extent the training system, the labour markets and the structure of industries continue to be determined by the institutional and societal framework in the country. However, at firm level, differences in training provision and use of skills seem to be considerably influenced by the management structure and organisation of the firm. It is highly unlikely that we would have found any significant trans-national organisational influences on personnel matters, owing both to the purely national circumference of almost all the case study SMEs and the fact that labour issues tend to be among the most devolved areas of decision making in any case. We were able to identify some (weak) trends towards convergence, mainly the increased use of the International Standard Organisation (ISO) quality assurance standards in both countries and more extensive use of innovative working practices such as team-working (see also Kelleher and Lee, 1993). However, on the whole, each of our three sectors presented a very different picture at both micro and macro levels in each country, and give some sustenance to Jobert's (1996) argument that the 'societal effect' approach may give insufficient weight to factors creating diversity within nations.

The regional dimension

Our project also had a strong regional component. The selection of the regions determined the kinds of comparisons which could be made and thus ultimately the character of the research which could be conducted. South Wales was chosen for two reasons. Firstly, it combines features of both the German regions we investigated: an area of declining 'heavy industries' with all the infrastructural problems and concerns this decline causes, and it is an area which has seen a substantial growth particularly in the engineering and service sectors. Secondly, South Wales was selected for practical reasons: access to the field was relatively easy and inexpensive, and we were able to draw on local knowledge concerning the economic structure, policy framework and the education and training system. Choosing this region also had the advantage of being well connected with local training and skills providers and with other agencies closely involved in the development of the region.

We chose the German region of Nordrhein-Westfalen as a focus of our study because it represents an older industrial region with declining steel and coal industries, and in that regard, is comparable to South Wales. Baden-Wuerttemberg was chosen because its economic infrastructure includes a large engineering sector. Another important consideration was that these two regions also inhabit quite different positions in the national political framework in Germany. In a decentralised nation such as Germany, policies and practices can and do vary considerably from region to region. This is an important aspect considering that the German *national* skills and training framework is frequently held up as a contrast to, and as a model for, Britain. It was therefore one of the aims of this research to investigate regionally-specific influences on training and skills provision, a phenomenon already noted by some commentators (eg Rees, 1997). We found that there were two factors where the regional dimension played an important role: firstly, all three regions had distinctively different labour markets and, secondly, contrasting policy processes. The two German regions had a different economic structure and political history, both having a weighty impact on the local labour market, regional politics and policy making. For example, in traditionally left-wing Nordrhein-Westfalen there was considerable political pressure for trainees to spend more time in the vocational schools during their apprenticeship. Since the schools and their curriculum are the responsibility of each state rather than the federal government, this, of course, meant that the regional government attempted to obtain more control over the content and provision of the school-based part of the dual system.

The most pronounced difference between the regions concerned the labour market: in both South Wales and Baden-Wuerttemberg, the labour market(s) tended to be very localised with people unwilling to move or commute. In contrast, in Nordrhein-Westfalen, the labour force was much more mobile, particularly regarding commuting. Needless to say, these labour market structures had an impact on skills supply: in both the regions with a less mobile work force it was more difficult to recruit appropriate employees.

In terms of policy, Wales has been well served both by national funding formulas and by a number of agencies which have enabled it to compete successfully with other regions in Britain for inward investment. While the true costs of this policy remain obscure, the number of enterprises which require workers with new and different skill combinations has grown. Consequently this process has stimulated a discussion in the region about the existing character of the skills pool, about present and future requirements, and how policy makers and training providers can meet these demands. Our research suggests that particularly in engineering there is considerable demand for sound initial training, and training providers have reacted with increased provision in this sector.

The sectoral dimension

A third dimension of comparison concerned the three sectors in our research. This in some ways was the most difficult part of our study. Although engineering and construction are, to some extent, similar creatures, the care sector is structured in a totally different way and is far more heterogeneous. These contrasting sectors were chosen deliberately. The care sector was selected to introduce a public service and a gendered element into the research: a focus on manufacturing and construction alone was likely to produce an account of training and multi-skilling which is strongly male focused and dominated. It was therefore necessary to introduce variation into the investigation by selecting a female-dominated sector such as care.

Comparisons between all three sectors are therefore only meaningful to a very limited extent – individual phenomena can be described as being different but without an explanation of the reasons for the differences such comparisons remain misleading. Both the organisational and structural variations between the sectors are enormous. In engineering and construction all firms visited were either limited or private companies (in both countries) whereas in the care sector, provision in both countries was a differing mixture of charitably, privately, or state (local authority in the UK) owned organisations. Whereas, inevitably, engineering and construction firms followed a business ethic, some of the care organisations were run on charitable lines, even though all of them had to cover costs. It would be misleading simply to collate and present

the data from all three sectors as if these structural differences did not exist. For example, we found that by far and away the greatest amount of multi-skilling went on in residential care homes in Germany. The reasons for this can be found in the nature of the work and the demands on staff in this sector. Neither engineering nor construction workers are expected to possess a similar variety of skills to perform their jobs nor are they presented with such a multitude of different tasks – it is therefore the nature of the sector rather than an active approach to multi-skilling which explains the difference.

Conclusion

The most important and defining feature of this project was its international comparative element. We found that many of the differences obtained in our results were linked to the respective national systems and structures, although some issues seemed to depend more on organisational factors than national differences. We would thus probably have to isolate the cross-national variations in the research as the dominant variable, rather more so than the still present, but more submerged, influence of regional and sectoral components within the project. A partial exception to this observation is the structural differences between the care sector and the other two sectors, especially given the inter-regional differences in the two German states.

Methodologically, it seems likely that the attempt to match pairs of similar organisations cross-nationally may be more effectively managed through the presence of active research teams in each of the countries to be studied. Unusually for projects employing this method, the 'Training for multi-skilling' study managed this with the research team based in only one country. This allowed closer control over the fieldwork, and greater ability to utilise in the analysis and dissemination phases of the project the tacit knowledge which came from the researchers' familiarity with the fieldwork. The dangers identified by other writers of misunderstanding meanings derived within the context of another country's institutional structure were minimised by the fact that the project included researchers who were natives of each country. Yet our method of managing the fieldwork also caused a number of significant difficulties connected with the attempt to pursue such research at – to some extent – arm's length. Thus, the practical difficulties in conducting about one hundred interviews abroad by cold calling were formidable: with hindsight much time could have been saved by establishing contacts first and then organising interviews through these contacts. For us, this only happened in the care sector. There may well be definite lessons for other researchers intending to pursue a matched pair approach to learn from our experiences documented in this paper.

Acknowledgements

We acknowledge funding under the ESRC *Learning Society* project 'Training for multi-skilling: a comparison of British and German experience' (Grant no L123251020), awarded to a team from the Centre for Advanced Studies in the Social Sciences and the School of Education, University of Wales Cardiff under the direction of Professor Phil Cooke. We appreciate the helpful contributions and comments of participants at the ESRC Learning Society Comparative Dimension Conference, University of Bristol, 14-15 October 1997, at which an earlier version of this paper was presented.

References

Bennett, R.J., Wicks, P. and McCoshan, A. (1994) *Local empowerment and business services: Britain's experiment with Training and Enterprise Councils*, London: UCL Press.

Bolton, B., Bramley, A. and Jones, B. (1993) 'A cross-sectoral investigation of skills and training in engineering', Final report to the Joint Committee of the SERC/ESRC, Grant no GR/G57482, Bath: University of Bath.

Bryman, A. (ed) (1988) *Doing research in organizations*, London and New York: Routledge.

Buchanan, D., Boddy, D., McCalman, J. (1988) 'Getting in, getting out, and getting back', in A. Bryman (ed) *Doing research in organizations*, London and New York: Routledge.

Campbell, A., Sorge, A. and Warner, M. (1989) *Microelectronic product applications in Great Britain and West Germany: Skills, competence and training*, Aldershot: Avebury.

Foskett, D.J. (1979) *Introduction to comparative librarianship*, Bangalore: Sarada Ranagathan Endowment for Library Science.

Hantrais, L. and Mangen, S. (eds) (1996) *Cross-national research methods in the social sciences*, London: Pinter.

Jobert, A. (1996) 'Comparing education, training and employment in Germany, the United Kingdom and Italy', in L. Hantrais and S. Mangen (eds) *Cross-national research methods in the social sciences*, London: Pinter, pp 76-83.

Kelleher, M. and Lee, B. (1993) *Developing the common core in Ford Europe. A study of skills and training in Wales, Spain, France and Germany*, Working Paper No 5, Cardiff: Welsh Joint Education Committee.

Koehler, C. and Woodard, J. (1997) 'Systems of work and socio-economic structures: a comparison of Germany, Spain, France and Japan', *European Journal of Industrial Relations*, vol 3, no 1, pp 59-82.

Kohn, M.L. (1989) 'Cross-national research as an analytical strategy', in M.L. Kohn (ed) *Cross-national research in sociology*, London: Sage, pp 77-102.

Lane, C. (1989) *Management and labour in Europe*, Aldershot: Edward Elgar.

Lawrence, P. (1988) 'In another country', in A. Bryman (ed) *Doing research in organizations*, London and New York: Routledge.

Mason, G. and Wagner, K. (1994) 'Innovation and the skill mix: chemicals and engineering', *National Institute Economic Review*, no 148, pp 61-72.

Maurice, M., Sellier, F. and Silvestre, J.-J. (1986) *The social foundations of industrial power*, Cambridge, MA: MIT Press.

Maurice, M., Sorge, A, and Warner, M. (1980) 'Societal differences in organizing manufacturing units: a comparison of France, West Germany and Great Britain', *Organization Studies*, vol 1, no 1, pp 59-86.

Meil, P. (1992) 'Stranger in paradise – an American's perspective on German industrial sociology', in N. Altmann, C. Koehler and P. Meil (eds) *Technology and work in German industry*, London: Routledge, pp 12-25.

Mueller, F. (1992) 'Flexible working practices in engine plants: evidence from the European automobile industry', *Industrial Relations Journal*, vol 23, pp 191-204.

Mueller, F. (1994a) 'Societal effect, organizational effect and globalization', *Organization Studies*, vol 15, no 3, pp 407-28.

Mueller, F. (1994b) 'Teams between hierarchy and commitment: change strategies and the "internal environment"', *Journal of Management Studies*, vol 31, no 3, pp 383-403.

O'Reilly, J. (1996) 'Theoretical considerations in cross-national employment research', *Sociological Research Online*, vol 1, no 1.

Patton, M.Q. (1987) *How to use qualitative methods in evaluation*, Newbury Park: Sage.

Rainbird, H. (1996) 'Negotiating a research agenda for comparisons of vocational training', in L. Hantrais and S. Mangen (eds) *Cross-national research methods in the social sciences*, London: Pinter, pp 109-19.

Rees, G. (1997) 'Vocational education and training and regional development: an analytical framework', *Journal of Education and Work*, vol 10, no 2, pp 341-9.

Rheingold, H. (1988) *They have a word for it*, Los Angeles: Tarcher.

Robinson, P. (1984) 'Languages in data collection: difficulties with diversity', *Journal of the Market Research Society*, vol 26, no 2, pp 159-69.

Rose, M. (1985) 'Universalism, culturalism and the Aix group: promise and problems of a societal approach to economic institutions', *European Sociological Review*, vol 1, no 1, pp 65-83.

Scott, P. and Kellcher, M. (1996) 'Convergence *and* fragmentation? Vocational training within the European Union', *European Journal of Education*, vol 31, no 4, pp 463-81.

Sorge, A., Hartmann, G., Nicholas, I. and Warner, M. (1983) *Microelectronics and manpower in manufacturing: Applications of computer numerical control in Great Britain and West Germany*, Aldershot: Gower.

Sorge, A. and Warner, M. (1986) *Comparative factory organisation. An Anglo-German comparison of management and manpower in manufacturing*, Aldershot: Gower.

Steedman, H. (1988) 'Vocational training in France and Britain: mechanical and electrical craftsman', *National Institute Economic Review*, no 126, pp 57-70.

Steedman, H., Mason, G. and Wagner, K. (1991) 'Intermediate skills in the workplace: deployment, standards and supply in Britain, France and Germany', *National Institute Economic Review*, no 136, pp 60-76.

Wiegand, A.J. (1985) *Erfolgreiche Bibliotheksarbeit in Sparzeiten: Ziele, Aufgaben und Planungskonzepte im Internationalen Vergleich – Ein Werkstattbereicht*, Gütersloh: Bertelsmannstiftung.